THE CHILDREN'S ATLAS OF

Scientific Discoveries
and Inventions

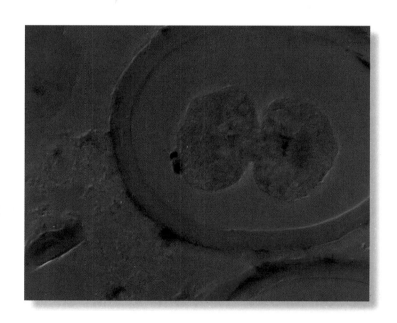

THE CHILDREN'S ATLAS OF

Scientific Discoveries and Inventions

ANDREW DUNN

The Millbrook Press
Brookfield, Ct

A QUARTO BOOK

First published in the United States of America in 1997 by
The Millbrook Press, Inc.
2 Old New Milford Road, Brookfield, Connecticut 06804

Library of Congress Cataloging-in-Publication Data

Dunn, Andrew.
   The children's atlas of scientific discoveries and inventions / Andrew Dunn
Summary: the earliest discoveries of humans and the flights of imagination
which brought about the most technologically advanced inventions of
the 20th century

     p.   cm.
   "A Quarto book."
   Includes bibliographical references and index.
   ISBN 0-7613-0220-4 (lib. bdg.). - - ISBN 0-7613-0241-7 (pbk.)
   1. Discoveries in science - - History - - 20th century - - Chronology -
- Juvenile literature. 2. Inventions - - History - - 20th century -
- Chronology - - Juvenile literature. I. Title.
   Q180.55.D57D86 1996
   509 - - dc20

                 96-38358
                 CIP
                 AC

This book was designed and produced by Quarto Children's Books Ltd,
The Fitzpatrick Building, 188 – 194 York Way, London N7 9QP

Creative Director Louise Jervis
Senior Art Editor Nigel Bradley
Project Editor Simon Beecroft
Editors Arianne Burnette and Louisa Sommerville
Page make up Nik Morley
Picture Managers Pernilla Nissen and Su Alexander
Assistant Editor Asha Kalbag
Researcher Rebecca Evans
Indexer Hilary Bird

Illustrations by
Julian Baker (maps), Peter Evans, Roger Hutchins, Kevin Jones Associates, Eugene Osborne

Manufactured by Centre Media, London
Printed by Star Standard Industries (Pte) Ltd, Singapore

CONTENTS

INTRODUCTION
Out of Africa 6 Early Science 8

SECTION ONE
Technology and the Birth of Ideas

Technology and the Birth of Ideas *10* Farming *12*
Time *14* Metals *16* Glass *18* Magnetism and Electricity *20*
The Nature of Light *22* Gravity *24* The Atom *26*
Oxygen *28* Plastics *30* Radioactivity and Invisible Rays *32*
Moving Continents *34* The Laser *36* Nuclear Power *38*

SECTION TWO
Communications and Travel

Communications and Travel *40* Writing *42*
Paper and Printing *44* Ships and Navigation *46*
Steam Power *48* Internal-Combustion Engine *50*
Powered Flight *52* The Bicycle *54* Telegraph and Telephone *56*
Photography and Film *58* Radio and Television *60*
Transistors and the Microchip *62* The Digital Revolution *64*

SECTION THREE
Learning About Life

Learning About Life *66* History of Medicine *68* The Living Cell *70*
Evolution *72* Genetics *74* DNA *76* Fighting Disease *78* Surgery *80*

SECTION FOUR
Astronomy and Cosmology

Astronomy and Cosmology *82* The Solar System *84*
Space Travel *86* Satellites *88* The Big Bang! *90*

Glossary 92
Index 95

Out of Africa

FROM THE EARLIEST TIMES, people have been discovering and inventing new things in an effort to understand the world around them. Each generation of scientists, inventors, and thinkers has built on the ideas and breakthroughs of preceding generations, so that even the earliest discoveries continue to influence our lives today.

Discovery versus invention

Discovery and invention are not the same thing. A discovery reveals something that already exists in the world, but that people were unaware of – such as magnetism, antibiotics, or atoms. An invention is something that is created for the first time – such as a mousetrap or a bicycle. Invention can also mean taking something that exists (such as a wooden log) and using it in a new way (as an axle, for instance).

◄ *Cave painting is one of the earliest known art forms. On the walls of these caves in southern France, artists painted the animals they hunted, using minerals to make the paints and animal fat to make the colors stick.*

Early progress

Exactly when humans began discovering and inventing is not known, but progress came very slowly at first. About 2,500,000 years ago, our distant ancestors in Africa were using simple stone tools, which they refined very gradually into blades, chisels, and axes.

About 40,000 years ago, people made quite sophisticated stone tools, with wood or bone handles. Later still, metal tools, made first of bronze (a mixture of copper and tin) and then of iron, were introduced. These technologies developed at different times in different places.

▼ *Early peoples learned how to use tools as weapons to hunt the animals that provided them with the meat, skins, and fur that were essential for their survival in colder climates. Here stampeding buffaloes are driven over a cliff with spears and clubs in a buffalo jump.*

DISCOVERING FIRE

At some point, probably about 750,000 years ago, the ancestors of modern man discovered how to tame fire. This meant they could cook food and migrate to and live in colder places around the world.

▶ *An early method of starting a fire involved a leather bow, three pieces of wood, and friction.*

The mouthpiece is used to hold the tool steady.

The bow is turned very fast.

Friction eventually creates sparks of fire.

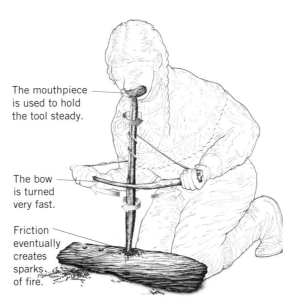

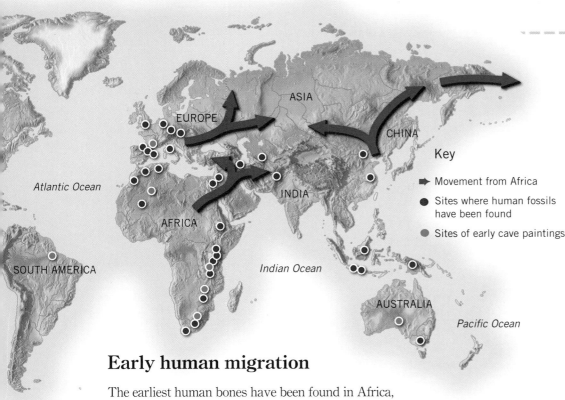

TOOLS

Our early ancestors showed great skill and ingenuity when it came to making tools. First they used familiar materials such as wood, bone, and stone. Later they made tools from the metals they discovered – bronze and iron.

❶ To make an ax head, a piece of flint was trimmed to the right shape.

❷ Then a rock was used to carve the ax head.

❸ The finishing touches were added with a bone hammer.

Key

➡ Movement from Africa

● Sites where human fossils have been found

● Sites of early cave paintings

Early human migration

The earliest human bones have been found in Africa, suggesting that this is where human life began. Early humans then spread into southern Asia about a million years ago and to northern Europe and the Americas about 70,000-10,000 years ago.

▶ *Early civilizations achieved great feats of engineering when building their temples, pyramids, and fortresses. Here Assyrians maneuver a huge statue of a human-headed bull into place, using rollers and levers.*

STONEHENGE

This famous megalithic monument on Salisbury Plain in England dates from about 2800 B.C. The largest stones are 18 feet (5.5 meters) high and weigh 26 tons. Some of them were brought great distances on wooden rollers.

▲ *Stonehenge may have been an early form of calendar.*

Early Science

U NTIL ABOUT 10,000 YEARS AGO, humans were hunter-gatherers, living where there was natural shelter and eating what they could find or catch. Gradually people began to exchange goods and develop regular trade routes. The first towns were built on the crossroads of these trade routes. Over time, people also became farmers when they began domesticating animals and cultivating plants for food and clothing.

Societies

Bigger, more organized groups of people came together to form societies. As a result, people could share the tasks that were necessary for their survival. This encouraged advances in technology, art, and science, and progress became more rapid.

The spread of ideas

Ideas rarely stayed in one place for long. As people traveled and traded with each other, interesting discoveries and inventions passed from town to town and from one civilization to another, from Sumer, the Indus Valley, Ancient Egypt, Greece, and Rome to the rest of the world.

NORTH AMERICA

Atlantic Ocean

SOUTH AMERICA

Civilization and science

The map shows the important regions where scientific thought developed and spread.

❑ Mesopotamia

◼ Indus Valley Civilization

◼ Ancient China

◼ Ancient Egypt

◼ Ancient Greece

◻ Ancient Rome

Stylus

Pigments

Egyptian writing desk

▼ *Mohenjo-Daro was the capital of the Indus Valley Civilization, which flourished from about 2500 to 1600 B.C. The city shows evidence of advanced town planning.*

▲ *Ancient Egyptian scribes at work. Modern archeologists have been able to use the detailed records made by scribes to learn much about this early great civilization.*

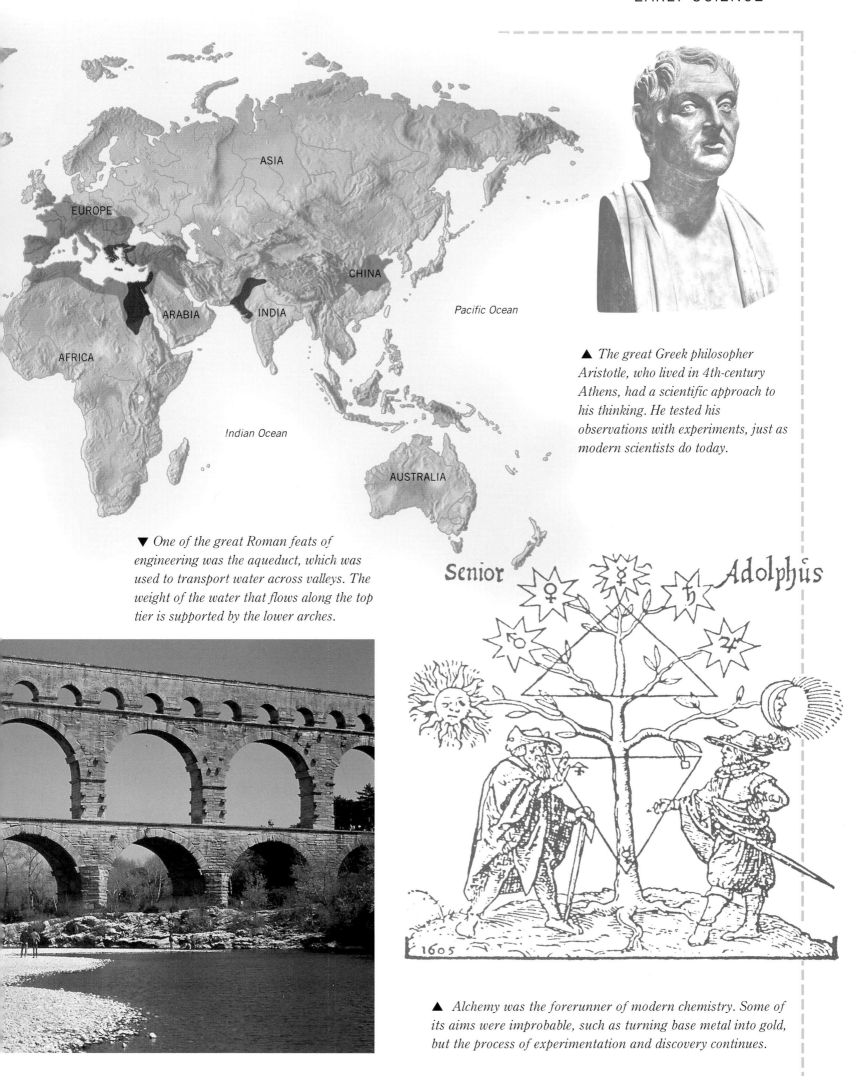

ASIA

EUROPE

CHINA

AFRICA

ARABIA

INDIA

Pacific Ocean

Indian Ocean

AUSTRALIA

▲ *The great Greek philosopher Aristotle, who lived in 4th-century Athens, had a scientific approach to his thinking. He tested his observations with experiments, just as modern scientists do today.*

▼ *One of the great Roman feats of engineering was the aqueduct, which was used to transport water across valleys. The weight of the water that flows along the top tier is supported by the lower arches.*

Senior

Adolphus

1605

▲ *Alchemy was the forerunner of modern chemistry. Some of its aims were improbable, such as turning base metal into gold, but the process of experimentation and discovery continues.*

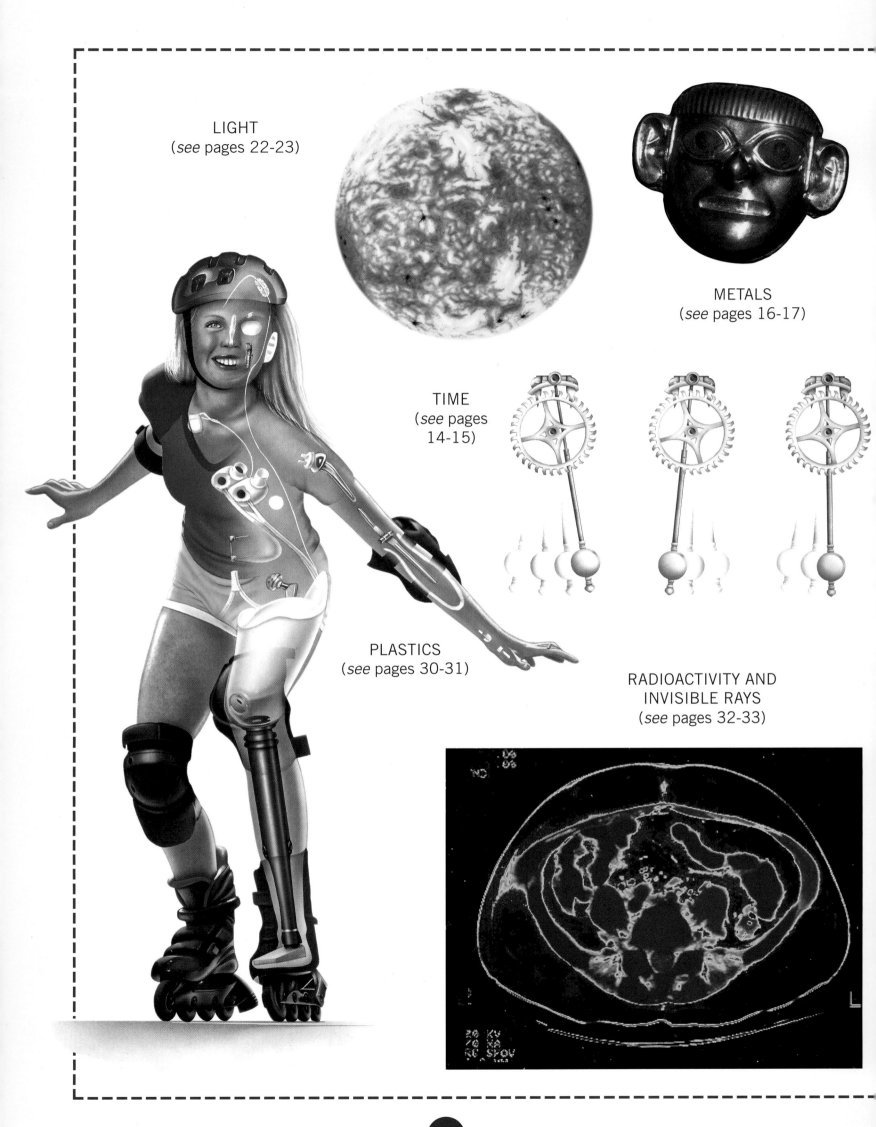

LIGHT
(*see* pages 22-23)

METALS
(*see* pages 16-17)

TIME
(*see* pages 14-15)

PLASTICS
(*see* pages 30-31)

RADIOACTIVITY AND
INVISIBLE RAYS
(*see* pages 32-33)

TECHNOLOGY AND THE BIRTH OF IDEAS

The first great inventions of our distant ancestors were the tools they used to hunt and grow food with. The use of tools and the ability to control fire were the first steps toward a scientific understanding.

Gradually people also learned how to measure time, use metal, and make glass. They began to understand naturally occurring phenomena such as electricity, light, and gravity. They also studied the substances that make life on Earth possible, such as atoms and oxygen, and how the Earth's surface has changed over time.

As scientific ideas and discoveries began to explain the unknown, new technological breakthroughs became possible. For example, the creation of plastics required an understanding of heat processes and atoms, while the invention of the laser depended upon knowledge about light and atoms. Studying the atomic nucleus also brought about the discovery of radioactivity and led to the use of nuclear power.

This section explores some of the many connections between scientific ideas, or theories, and technology, the application of science.

Farming

THE EARLIEST PEOPLE hunted and scavenged for food. But about 10,000 years ago, an agricultural revolution began in the fertile valleys of the rivers Euphrates and Tigris in Mesopotamia (modern Iraq), the Nile in Egypt, and the Jordan in the Middle East (now Lebanon, Syria, and Israel).

People began organized farming by tending herds of animals and following them wherever they went. In this way, wild animals such as cattle, sheep, and pigs became domesticated. People also realized they could increase their food yields if they chose crops and animals that thrived in a particular area. They cultivated wild mountain grasses such as rice, wheat, and barley. Natural clearings and open land were used for farming – and when farmers needed more land, they cleared huge areas of forest. They tilled the soil with digging sticks hardened by fire, and used the animals to tread in the seed. Sophisticated ways of storing and preserving food were developed, such as keeping grain in pits called silos and in big granaries.

Wild blueberries

Wild plums

▲ *Wild fruits and grains were important crops for early farmers. They learned how to tend them in order to produce more food.*

The spread of agriculture

This map shows the spread of agriculture from the Middle East and Mesopotamia toward western Europe from about 8000 B.C. to 5000 B.C.

TURKEY

Mediterranean Sea

EGYF

▼ *Maize was first cultivated by farmers in North America, where it grew naturally. Each color has a different taste.*

▼ *The Middle Ages (A.D. 500-1500) saw the development of plows that were heavy and strong enough to slice through the thick soils of western Europe.*

Improving farming methods
One of the most important early developments in farming was irrigation – the transporting of water from rivers to fields farther away. This invention was particularly crucial in Egypt and the Middle East, where there are long periods of drought. The Sumerians, who lived in Mesopotamia, were the first to dig irrigation canals from rivers to fields. Over the centuries, they transformed desert into green pastures and orchards – and the first great civilization was born.

Farming inventions since then have aimed at improving harvests and making the work less hard. The 18th century in particular brought a new agricultural revolution, when inventions such as machines for planting seeds allowed more food to be grown and harvested. The greater use of machinery and chemicals, as well as intensive methods, in the 20th century has improved crop yields even more. Modern agriculture is potentially capable of feeding the entire population of the planet. Hunger and starvation around the world are generally the result of complicated economics and politics, not farming.

◀ *Ancient Egyptian farmers turned the loose, sandy soils of the region with light plows called scratch plows.*

▶ *Iron, which had been invented in the Middle East in about 1100 B.C., was a widespread metal in the medieval period, used to improve farming tools.*

The **scythe** was a sharp metal blade used to harvest grain, such as wheat and barley.

The **hoe** was used to loosen the earth in preparation for planting seeds.

The **flail** was used to beat the grain in order to separate the useful part from the husk.

The **seed bag** was used to hold the seeds when sowing the new crops.

Black Sea

Caspian Sea

SYRIA

M I D D L E   E A S T

MESOPOTAMIA

Extent of agriculture

■ 8000 B.C.

■ 7000 B.C.

■ 6000 B.C.

□ 5000 B.C.

Persian Gulf

▼ *Modern farming is mechanically regulated to produce enormous yields. In this Japanese hydroponics vegetable factory, crops are grown in gravel, through which nutrient-rich water is pumped.*

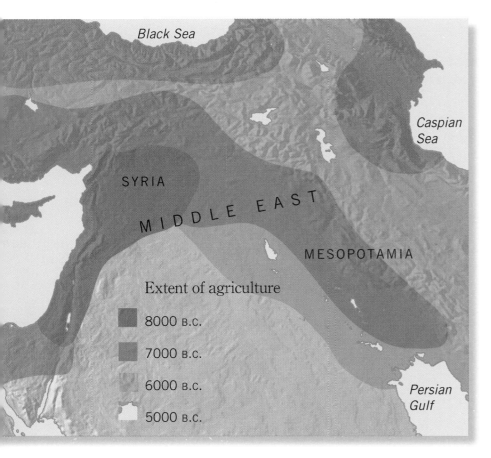

Empty field

Wheat or rye

Barley, oats, or peas

Clover

Barley

Root crops

Wheat

Medieval system

19th-century system

CROP ROTATION

In the Middle Ages, it was discovered that fields could be kept fertile by changing the crops grown on them and occasionally leaving one empty so that it could recover its nutrients. (Most plants use up nutrients in the soil.)

In the 19th century, four-field crop rotation relaced the three-field method. Instead of leaving one field empty, clover or turnips were planted in the fourth field. These crops were fed to animals, whose manure improved soil quality.

Time

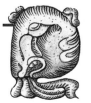

▶ *These Mayan images, or glyphs, represent some of the months in the Mayan calendar.*

T HE PASSING OF TIME WAS FIRST understood by early people in terms of natural cycles: day and night, the seasons, and the monthly phases of the moon. Farmers used this understanding of time when planting and harvesting crops. In countries where there is a rainy season, early farmers could predict when the rains would come.

People also learned to interpret the night sky, in particular the movement of the planets against the background of the stars, which did not appear to move. The ancient Chinese and Babylonians (from Mesopotamia) became the first skilled astronomers. They recorded and were able to predict solar eclipses. The Egyptians invented the first calendar 7,000 years ago. It had 12 months of 30 days each, making 360 days in a year. When this calendar drifted away from the real seasons, five feast days were added to make the 365-day year used today.

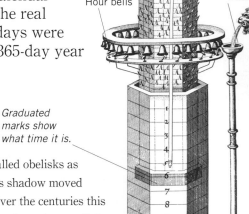

Hour bells

Water

Graduated marks show what time it is.

EARLY TIMEKEEPERS

By 3,500 years ago, the Egyptians were using tall pillars called obelisks as primitive sundials. As the sun crossed the sky, the obelisk's shadow moved around its base, and it could be measured on the ground. Over the centuries this was improved to the "gnomon" in ancient Greece and China. A garden sundial is a gnomon. It takes account of the time of year and the changing angles of the sun. A sundial can be surprisingly accurate, but only when the sun shines.

▲ *The first mechanical clocks were built in public places such as monasteries and cathedrals. This one hangs in Wells Cathedral in England and was built in 1392. The first portable clocks were developed in Germany from about 1500.*

Clock face

Gnomon

▲ *Water clocks were devised about 2,700 years ago. They relied on water dripping at a slow rate into or out of a container where the time could be read from graduated hour marks.*

▶ *The Italian mathematician Galileo Galilei noticed in about 1580 that a pendulum "kept" time: it swung with a regular beat. In 1656 the Dutch astronomer Christiaan Huygens put a pendulum into a clock, which improved accurate clock-making.*

Anchor

Pallet

Tooth

❶ *In a mechanical clock, an escape wheel (driven by a spring) turns clockwise, giving the pendulum a nudge on each swing so it does not stop.*

Escape wheel, turned by a spring (not shown)

❷ *A tooth of the escape wheel pushes one pallet of the anchor until the other pallet catches on another tooth (shown in ❸).*

❸ *This back-and-forth movement of the anchor keeps the pendulum swinging.*

▲ *In about 1500, a German in Nuremberg began making small clocks driven by wound-up springs – the first portable clocks or pocket watches.*

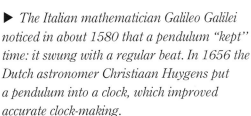

Pendulum

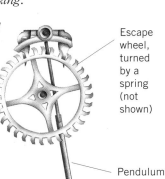

Weight

ANCIENT CALENDARS

As long as 7,000 years ago, the Ancient Egyptians had a calendar with twelve months. This Mayan calendar dates from between the 4th and 10th centuries A.D.. Through its intricate workings, an accurate record was kept of the days and months.

There are three interlocking wheels that make up the Mayan calendar.

The 20 glyphs on this wheel represent the 20 days in a Mayan month.

These 18 glyphs represent the 18 months in the calendar.

The day and the month are shown here.

Time zones

The world is divided into 24 time zones, each representing one hour in the 24-hour clock. This time zone map shows the time in different parts of the world.

	Christian	Muslim	Jewish	Hindu
Spring	Easter	Eid Al-Fitr (the end of Ramadan)	Passover Shavuot (Pentecost)	Holi
Summer	Pentecost Corpus Christi	Eid Al-Agha (pilgrimage to Mecca)		Ganesh Chaturthi
Autumn	Harvest festival Thanksgiving	Eid Milad-un-Nabi (Birth of Muhammad)	Rosh Hashanah (New Year) Yom Kippur	Divali
Winter	Christmas		Sukkot Hanukkah	Vasanta Panchami

FESTIVALS

Festivals are celebrated all over the world and have been for thousands of years. They are another way of marking the passing of time in the annual calendar. Above are some of the most well-known festivals in the world's major religions, and the seasons in which they are celebrated.

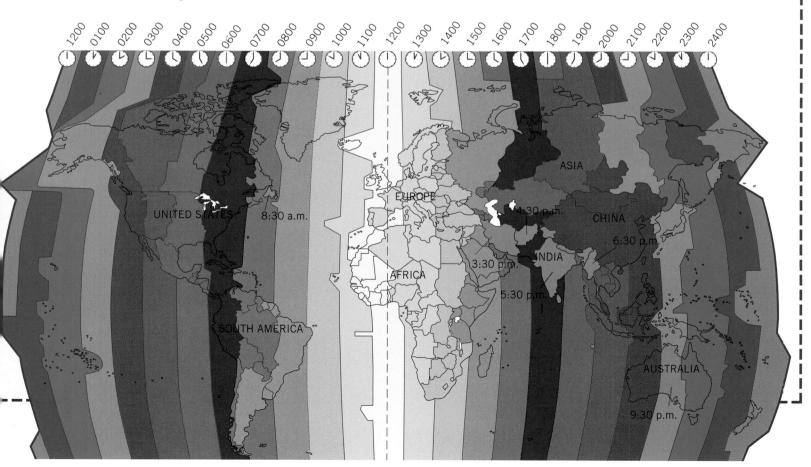

1200 0100 0200 0300 0400 0500 0600 0700 0800 0900 1000 1100 1200 1300 1400 1500 1600 1700 1800 1900 2000 2100 2200 2300 2400

UNITED STATES 8:30 a.m.

EUROPE

ASIA

CHINA 6:30 p.m.

INDIA 5:30 p.m.

3:30 p.m.

4:30 p.m.

AFRICA

SOUTH AMERICA

AUSTRALIA 9:30 p.m.

Metals

A MAJOR ADVANCE IN TECHNOLOGY was the use of metals. Wood, bone, and stone tools had been used for thousands of years, but pure metals were not easily found. The earliest known metal ornaments were carved from natural metal nuggets about 7,000 years ago. Most metals, however, are found in combination with other elements in rock ores, and these must be separated in order to obtain the pure form. This was done by heating rock ores to high temperatures. The pure metal could then be shaped and molded.

In about 4000 B.C., copper was first made by heating certain colored rocks in a fire with charcoal. Copper on its own is soft and corrodes too easily to be of much use except for ornaments. But it was then discovered that if copper is mixed with a little tin, it becomes a much harder metal – bronze – which is strong enough to make useful weapons and tools.

The spread of metals

Bronze and iron were first used in Thailand, in the Far East. The skills then spread to the Middle East, and from there to Europe. The Italian explorer Christopher Columbus took iron with him to the Americas when he crossed the Atlantic in 1492. Bronze, however, was already known.

Origins of the Iron Age

Iron was known early on, but extracting it from its ores took much higher temperatures than had been needed to extract copper. For centuries it was a precious, expensive metal. Then, in about 1400 B.C., the Hittite people of Asia Minor (modern Turkey) discovered that blowing air by a bellows into a furnace produced a hotter fire, which smelted iron from its ores. They made iron swords which could slice through bronze weapons.

THE RAW MATERIAL

Galena, shown here, is the ore of lead.

Certain colored rocks, called ores, contain metals mixed with other elements. These elements are removed in order to produce purer, stronger metal.

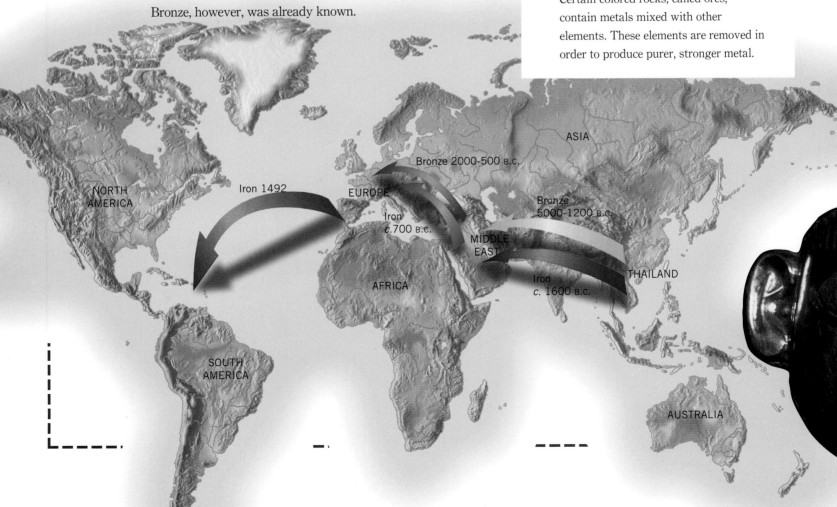

NORTH AMERICA

SOUTH AMERICA

EUROPE

AFRICA

ASIA

MIDDLE EAST

THAILAND

AUSTRALIA

Iron 1492

Bronze 2000-500 B.C.

Iron c. 700 B.C.

Bronze 5000-1200 B.C.

Iron c. 1600 B.C.

MAKING STEEL

In 1856, English engineer Henry Bessemer invented a process that made steel from iron. The "Bessemer converter" adds oxygen to iron in order to burn off most of the impurity carbon, leaving only a tiny amount that strengthens the metal. Steel is much stronger than iron and is used for car bodies, ships, boats, and more.

Impurities escape here.

❷ Converter is raised and given a blast of hot

Hot air is blasted in here.

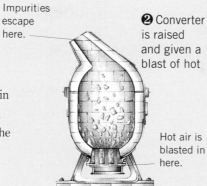

❶ Molten iron is added to the riveted vessel (the Bessemer converter).

Molten iron

❸ The molten steel is poured out.

▶ Iron ore being smelted in Central Asia in the late 19th century. Six men increase the draft with bellows.

▶ Steel being manufactured in England in the 19th century using a Bessemer converter.

▶ The development of steel allowed tall buildings, such as these skyscrapers in New York, to be built. Steel provides the supporting structure.

▲ This U.S. air force plane is made of aluminum, which is lighter than steel. The American Charles Hall was the first to discover how to process aluminium cheaply, in 1886. The cockpit is strengthened with a very expensive and heavy metal called titanium.

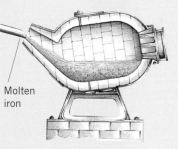

◀ Gold is a soft metal used by many early civilizations to make precious ornaments, such as this South American mask.

Glass

THE OLDEST KNOWN PIECES of glass are glass beads from Mesopotamia (now Iraq) and ancient Egypt, dating from about 2500 B.C. The first vessels were sculpted from solid blocks, and it was another 1,000 years before the Egyptians were molding glass and decorating it with blobs of colored glass.

Roman glassmaking

A new method of manufacture adopted by the Romans was glass blowing, in which air was blown into a blob of molten glass to form a hollow center. The Romans made the first window panes – they were simply crude lumps of greenish glass, held in small frames.

▶ *Glass can be used to make optical fibers – long strands of glass, thinner than human hair, that carry laser light. Today, most telephone calls and other communication signals are carried by pulses of light along optical fibers.*

Medieval secrets

Glass making declined after A.D. 200, but was revived in Venice, Italy, in the 15th century. So secret were the methods used that glass workers were forbidden to leave the city. But by the 16th century the secret had escaped, and soon glass was being made throughout Europe.

Glass is made from sand heated to about 1,562°F (850°C), and mixed with soda ash and limestone. Today, there are many different types, including heat resistant glass, photochromic glass that darkens in bright light, glass fabrics for protective clothing, and glass that protects against X-rays.

FLOAT GLASS

In the 1960s, the Pilkington glass-manufacturing company in England invented a new method of making large panes of high quality, flat glass. Known as the float glass process, it involves floating molten glass over molten tin to form a continuous, almost perfectly flat, sheet of glass. The temperature is carefully controled as the glass cools so that the glass does not crack before it is finally cut to size by the diamond-tipped cutting machine.

▼ *Invented in 1821, the split mold is used today in automatic bottle-making machines. Molten glass is dropped into the mold* ❶ *until it reaches the correct level* ❷. *Hot air is then forced inside the mold* ❸, *pushing the glass to the edges. The jar is left to cool* ❹ *before being removed* ❺.

▶ *Here, 19th century glass blowers are seen using a blowing iron, which has a mouthpiece at one end and a knob for holding the molten glass at the other.*

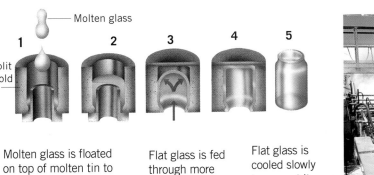

— Molten glass

Split mold

1   2   3   4   5

Molten glass is floated on top of molten tin to give a very flat surface.

Flat glass is fed through more rollers.

Flat glass is cooled slowly to prevent it cracking.

Glass cut to size with a diamond-tip cutter.

Raw materials (mainly sand) are fed into a furnace, which is heated to over 2550°F (1400°C).

Molten glass is fed through rollers.

Furnace where glass is melted

Molten tin in float bath

Cooling chamber

▼ *Glass-blowing has been used since Roman times to make glass objects. Until the mid-19th century, it was even used in the production of flat glass for windows. Today, skilled craft-workers continue to use the technique to make special, high quality pieces.*

VENETIAN GLASS

As well as reviving Roman glass-making skills, the Venetians developed many new techniques, including a way of making a bright, clear glass that became highly valued throughout Europe. Venetian glass was often highly decorated and richly colored. The color was produced by adding metal oxides to the glass, such as cobalt for blue and chromium for yellow or green.

▶ *Today, early Venetian glass, such as this chandelier, is much prized by collectors.*

◀ *A continuous strip of flat glass passes over the rollers in a float glass factory.*

Important centers of glassmaking

The earliest glassworks, active in 1400 B.C., was discovered at el-Armarna in Egypt in 1894. By 40 B.C., glass was blown in Syria. The first good-quality glass was made in Alexandria, in Egypt, and in ancient Rome. In the 15th century A.D., Venice became a world center for glass-making.

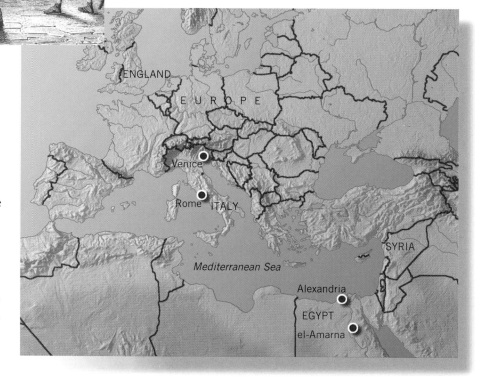

Magnetism and Electricity

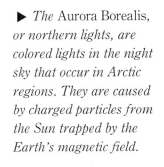

PEOPLE HAVE KNOWN ABOUT the effects of electricity and magnetism since ancient times, but it is only in the last 150 years or so that these two important phenomena have been understood and put to widespread use.

The ancient Greeks knew that if amber (fossilized pine resin) was rubbed with fur it would attract feathers and fluff, but they did not know why. We now know that this happens because the amber has become electrically "charged" due to the buildup of electrons (*see* page 26) on its surface. This kind of electric charge is called *static* (still) electricity. Most of the electricity we use today, however, is *moving* electricity, in the form of a flow, or current, of electrons.

The ancient Greeks also discovered a type of black stone, called a lodestone, that attracted metal objects. This was a naturally occurring magnet. It is now understood that, like electricity, magnetism is caused by electrons. As they spin around the nucleus of the atom, the electrons create tiny magnetic fields (areas of magnetism). Usually, these magnetic forces are randomly arranged throughout a substance, and have no overall effect, but if they can be made to line up, as happens in a bar magnet, the substance becomes magnetized.

▶ *The* Aurora Borealis, *or northern lights, are colored lights in the night sky that occur in Arctic regions. They are caused by charged particles from the Sun trapped by the Earth's magnetic field.*

POLES APART

The Earth's magnetic north pole is not in the same place as the true North Pole, around which the Earth rotates. In fact, the magnetic pole varies slightly in position from year to year. Navigators therefore have to make slight adjustments to their compass readings to take this into account.

Axle drives generator to produce electricity

This multistage steam turbine is the most efficient type of turbine. It is able to extract nearly all the energy from the steam.

Magnetic lines of force

Magnetic north pole

▲ *Inside the Earth is a core of iron that acts like a huge magnet, creating a magnetic field around the Earth. As in all magnets, invisible lines of magnetic force stretch out between the ends, or poles, of the magnet.*

MAGNETS AND COMPASSES

The first compasses were lodestones hung from a thread. The magnetic lodestone would swivel around until it was lined up with the Earth's magnetic lines of force (see right), in which position it would be pointing north/south. A modern magnetic compass, although more sophisticated, acts in a similar way. It consists of a magnetic needle balanced on a central pivot.

▲ *A compass needle always points toward the Earth's magnetic north pole.*

Lodestone

THE DISCOVERY OF ELECTROMAGNETISM

▼ *In modern generators, an electric current is induced by turning, or rotating, an electromagnet inside a fixed coil or solenoid. The power to rotate the electromagnet comes from a turbine, which is itself driven by either water or steam. Turbines are used to produce 95% of the world's electricity.*

It had long been thought that there was a link between electricity and magnetism, but it was the pioneering work of English scientist Michael Faraday (1791-1867) that finally proved the connection. In 1831, he discovered that a magnetic force moving near to a coil of wire would make an electric current flow through the wire. Similarly, he found that an electric current creates a magnetic field around itself. This was the phenomenon of electromagnetism, which ultimately led to the development of the electricity generator, the public power supply, and the electric motor.

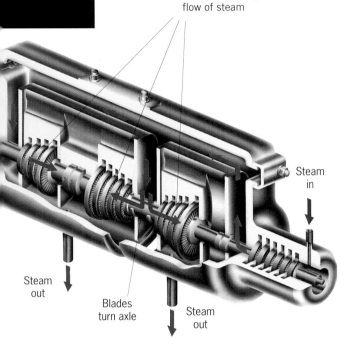

Fanlike blades, or vanes, turned by flow of steam

Steam in

Steam out

Blades turn axle

Steam out

▶ *Michael Faraday's laboratory in the Royal Institution in London, England.*

Moving magnet

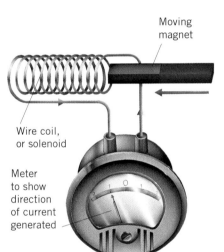

Wire coil, or solenoid

Meter to show direction of current generated

◀ *In one of his experiments, Faraday moved a bar magnet in and out of a large wire coil, or solenoid. He found that as the bar was moved into the solenoid, a current flowed in one direction. As the bar moved out again the current flowed the opposite way. But when the bar was stationary there was no current at all.*

The spread of magnetism

Magnetism was discovered in ancient China and the knowledge spread along an ancient trading route to the West. This route is known as the Silk Road because Chinese silks were important trading items.

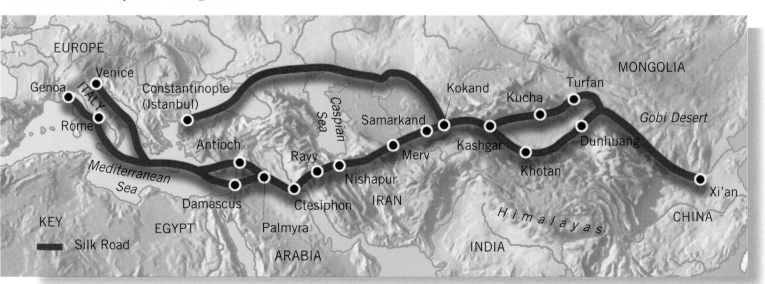

EUROPE

Genoa
Venice
ITALY
Rome

Constantinople (Istanbul)

Antioch

MONGOLIA

Turfan

Kokand
Kucha

Caspian Sea

Samarkand

Gobi Desert

Rayy

Merv

Kashgar

Dunhuang

Nishapur

Khotan

Mediterranean Sea

Damascus

Ctesiphon

IRAN

Himalayas

Xi'an

KEY

EGYPT

Palmyra

INDIA

CHINA

Silk Road

ARABIA

The Nature of Light

IN ANCIENT TIMES, people thought that their eyes sent out light, enabling them to see objects. It was an Arabic physicist known as Alhazen who first suggested 1,000 years ago that the reverse was true – that it is light *coming* from the object that allows us to see it.

A further step in our understanding of light was made in 1666, when the great British scientist Sir Isaac Newton discovered that sunlight could be split into a band of colors, which he called a spectrum. Newton believed that light is a stream of tiny particles, or "corpuscles," which travels very fast. His theory was consistent with the fact that light travels in straight lines, but did not explain how light is bent, or refracted, when it passes from air into glass or water.

Then, in 1680, Dutch scientist Christian Huygens suggested that light travels in waves (rather like the ripples in a pond), which would explain both refraction and light traveling in straight lines.

▶ *Light is a form of energy. It travels through the vacuum of empty space at 186,000 miles/sec (300,000 km/sec). Sunlight provides the energy for all life on Earth.*

ISAAC NEWTON

In 1666, Isaac Newton shone sunlight from a narrow slit in his curtain through a prism (a triangular block of glass) and onto a screen, forming a band of colors. Newton deduced that white light must be a mixture of different colors. We now know that each color has a different wavelength, which explains why the colors are refracted (bent) by different degrees as they pass through the prism.

White light

Prism

Violet
Indigo
Blue
Green
Yellow
Orange
Red

▲ *A prism refracts light and splits it into the seven colors of the spectrum – just like water droplets in the atmosphere split sunlight to form a rainbow.*

▼ *The camera obscura was an instrument used in the 18th and 19th centuries for drawing. Light from an object was projected through a tiny hole, or aperture, to form an image on a screen, just as light passing through the iris of the eye forms an image on the retina (back of the eye).*

▼ *Our Sun is part of the Milky Way galaxy – a giant group of about 100 billion stars, each giving off heat and light. Virtually all of our Earth's natural light comes from our nearest star, the Sun.*

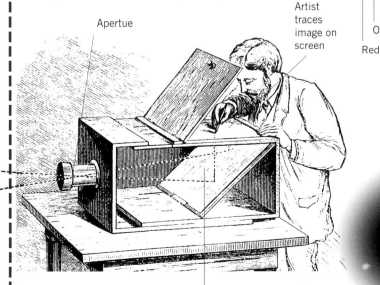

Apertue

Artist traces image on screen

Light from object

Image forms on screen

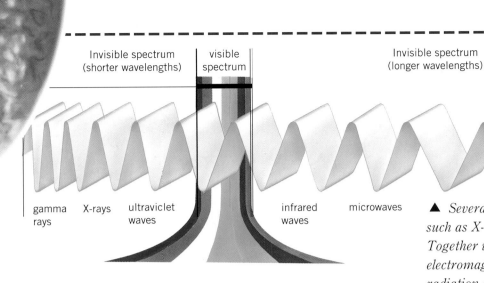

Invisible spectrum (shorter wavelengths) | visible spectrum | Invisible spectrum (longer wavelengths)

wavelength

radio waves

gamma rays | X-rays | ultraviclet waves | infrared waves | microwaves

Colors of the visible spectrum

▲ *Several forms of energy travel in waves – such as X-rays, radio waves, and microwaves. Together with light, they form what is called the electromagnetic spectrum. The different types of radiation (rays) have different wavelengths, ranging from fractions of an inch to many miles.*

Pioneers of Light

Light was studied by the Arabic physicist Alhazen in Cairo, Egypt. Isaac Newton worked in Cambridge, England, and Huygens worked in The Hague, Holland. Thomas Young lived in London.

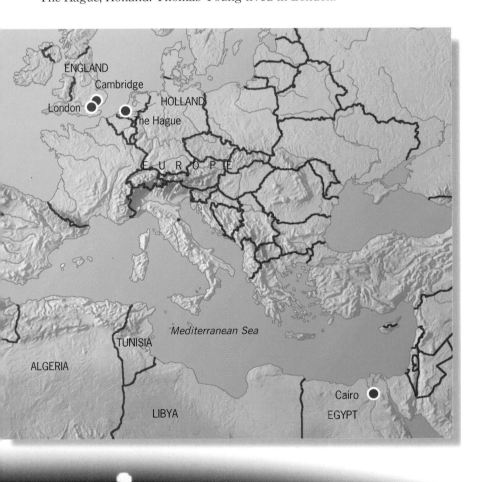

ENGLAND
Cambridge
London
HOLLAND
The Hague
E U R O P E
Mediterranean Sea
TUNISIA
ALGERIA
LIBYA
Cairo
EGYPT

YOUNG'S PROOF

Huygens had suggested that light travels in waves, but it was British physicist Thomas Young who proved it. In 1801, Young shone light through a series of narrow apertures to create two identical beams of light that he projected onto a screen (see below). Where the beams overlapped, they formed bands of light and dark on the screen. This could only be explained if light travels in waves. Where the waves from the two beams were in step they created a stronger light, but where they were out of step they canceled each other out and there was darkness.

Screen
Area of light and dark banding
Two overlapping beams of light
Two apertures
Single light beam
Screen
Single aperture
Single light source

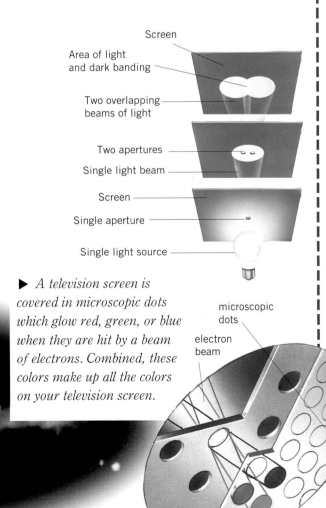

▶ *A television screen is covered in microscopic dots which glow red, green, or blue when they are hit by a beam of electrons. Combined, these colors make up all the colors on your television screen.*

microscopic dots
electron beam

Gravity

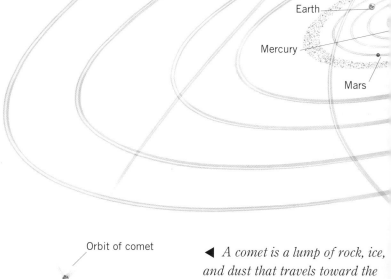

Earth

Mercury

Mars

WHY DOESN'T THE MOON FLY AWAY from the Earth, or the planets from the Sun? What holds everything in its place? Why do objects fall down to the ground and not up into the sky when they are dropped? The answer is gravity, a force that pulls all objects toward the ground. Without gravity everything on Earth would fly off into space.

Until the 16th century nobody understood how moving objects behave. Then the Italian scientist Galileo Galilei did experiments to show that falling objects accelerate at the same rate, no matter what they weigh – so, if there is no air resistance, a feather and a hammer dropped from an equal height would reach the ground at the same time. It is gravity that makes this happen.

Newton and gravity

In the 17th century Isaac Newton worked out the laws of gravity. The basic law is that gravity pulls all objects toward each other. The size of its force depends on the mass of the two objects, and how far apart they are. The more mass an object has, the stronger its gravitational pull. The Earth's mass is so much larger than the mass of other nearby objects in space, that it is usually only the Earth's gravity of which we are aware.

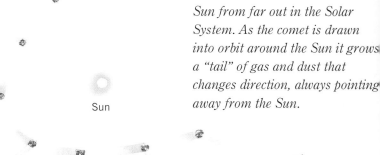

Orbit of comet

Sun

Comet

Tail

◄ *A comet is a lump of rock, ice, and dust that travels toward the Sun from far out in the Solar System. As the comet is drawn into orbit around the Sun it grows a "tail" of gas and dust that changes direction, always pointing away from the Sun.*

NEWTON AND THE APPLE

It is said that Newton was sitting in his garden in the English village of Woolsthorpe one day when he noticed an apple fall from a tree. It struck him that the force that pulled the apple from the tree to the ground may also extend into space. If so, then this force would also pull the Moon into orbit around the Earth. Eventually, he proved mathematically that the Earth and the other planets are kept in orbit around the Sun by gravity.

◄ *Newton did much of his thinking at his house after he and his fellow students were sent home from Cambridge University when a plague broke out.*

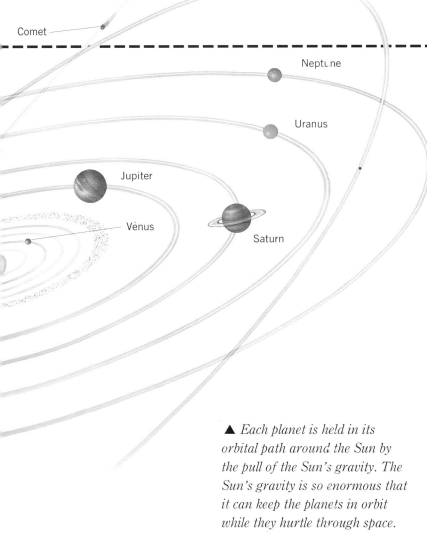

Comet

Neptune

Uranus

Jupiter

Venus

Saturn

▲ *Each planet is held in its orbital path around the Sun by the pull of the Sun's gravity. The Sun's gravity is so enormous that it can keep the planets in orbit while they hurtle through space.*

GRAVITY IN SPACE

Your weight and that of all objects is the pull of the Earth's gravity on the mass of your body. Your weight is only your weight on Earth. On the Moon, your mass would be exactly the same, but you would weigh much less because the Moon's gravitational force is much weaker. In a spacecraft out in space, where there is almost no gravity, you would be almost weightless.

▶ *Astronauts in space float freely because they are continuously falling, but moving forward at a speed that balances the pull of gravity.*

▼ *The Moon's gravity is lower than Earth's, yet it still affects our planet by causing tides. When it is overhead, the Moon's gravity pulls the water in the oceans, causing a high tide (below). As the Earth rotates, all places have high tides (and low tides, left) twice a day.*

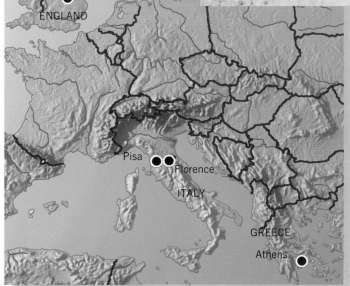

Woolsthorpe

ENGLAND

Pisa
Florence

ITALY

GREECE

Athens

The discoverers of gravity

The Greek philosopher Aristotle, who lived in Athens in Ancient Greece, was the first person to put forward theories about why objects move. His ideas were disproved by Galileo, who lived in Pisa and in Florence, Italy. Isaac Newton lived in Woolsthorpe in Lincolnshire, England.

The Atom

THE GREEK PHILOSOPHER Democritus (460-361 B.C.) was the first to put forward the idea that everything is made of tiny particles, which he called "atoms." In 1802, the English chemist John Dalton developed his atomic theory, suggesting that each chemical element was made of identical atoms, and that different elements were made up of different atoms. But was the atom the smallest particle?

The answer to this had to wait until 1897, when physicist J. J. Thomson proved the existence of electrons – tiny negatively charged particles that are smaller than atoms. He was succeeded in his work by Ernest Rutherford whose experiments showed that the atom is largely empty space, with a nucleus at the center – made of positively charged protons – and electrons in orbit around it. The modern picture of the atom was completed in 1930 by James Chadwick, who discovered a nuclear particle called a neutron.

▶ The atom as we know it today. It is made up of three main particles – protons, neutrons, and electrons. At the center is a nucleus containing neutrons and positively charged protons, about which orbit a series of negatively charged electrons. Electrons are not solid – they are fast-moving bundles of energy.

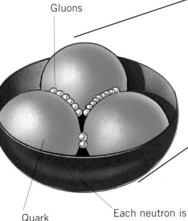

Gluons

Quark

Electron shell

Each neutron is made up of three quarks held together by gluons.

▲ When atomic particles collide, the paths made by electrons can be seen in special machines called cloud chambers.

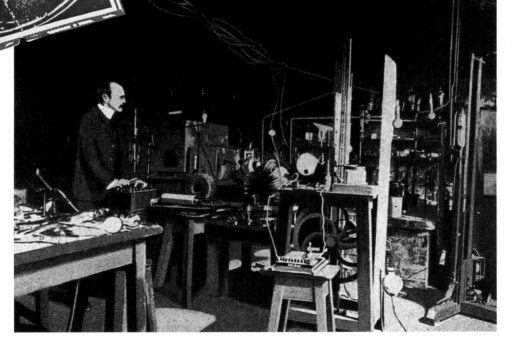

◀ British physicist, J. J. Thomson (1856-1940) in his laboratory at Cambridge University, England. His experiments with cathode rays led to the discovery of negatively charged atomic particles called electrons.

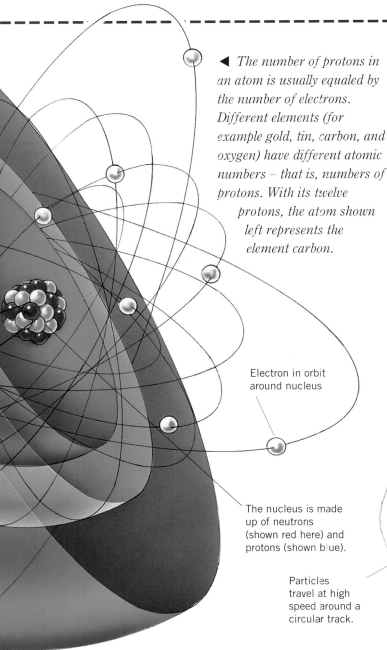

◀ *The number of protons in an atom is usually equaled by the number of electrons. Different elements (for example gold, tin, carbon, and oxygen) have different atomic numbers – that is, numbers of protons. With its twelve protons, the atom shown left represents the element carbon.*

Electron in orbit around nucleus

The nucleus is made up of neutrons (shown red here) and protons (shown blue).

Particles travel at high speed around a circular track.

SUBATOMIC PARTICLES

Current atomic research is concerned with the nature of "subatomic" particles – the tiny particles of which atomic particles, such as protons and electrons, are made. At the European Center for Nuclear Research (CERN) near Geneva, Switzerland, a vast particle accelerator, or atom smasher, is used to accelerate atomic particles to high speeds. The particles are then crashed into each other, producing smaller particles whose movements are tracked by electronic detectors. These and other experiments have revealed the existence of more than 200 subatomic particles, including quarks, which may be the smallest building blocks of the universe; gluons, which bind particles within the nucleus together; and photons, which make up a beam of light. Scientists are even hunting for something called a graviton, which may cause gravity.

▼ *The "atom smasher" at the CERN center near Geneva, Switzerland, where scientists are studying the nature of subatomic particles.*

Pioneers of the atom

John Dalton was a schoolteacher in Manchester, England. J. J. Thomson was a professor of physics at Cambridge University, in England. The New Zealander Ernest Rutherford studied at Cambridge and worked at McGill University in Canada and Manchester University, England.

▲ *At the CERN center powerful electromagnets are used to speed up the atomic particles as they travel around the circular track. By studying the smaller particles that are released when atomic particles collide, scientists have learned much about the structure of the atom.*

Oxygen

U NTIL ABOUT 400 YEARS AGO, air was thought of as a simple gas. It was only in the early 17th century, when the first experiments on gases were carried out, that people began to suspect that air was a mixture of different gases.

In 1774, an English chemist named Joseph Priestley discovered that bubbles of a colorless gas are given off when mercury oxide powder is heated. A candle burned more brightly in this gas, which made Priestley think it must be a special kind of air. In fact, he had discovered oxygen. A Swedish scientist, Carl Sheele, had discovered oxygen two years earlier, but had not published his results.

Priestley then traveled to Europe and met the French scientist Antoine Lavoisier in Paris. Lavoisier discovered that oxygen is the active part of air; it combines easily with other elements and is essential for combustion, or burning. All animals, even bacteria, depend upon oxygen to live. When taken into the body, it combines with other chemicals to produce energy.

▶ *The atmosphere at sea level contains enough oxygen for animals to live. The air becomes thinner at higher altitudes.*

The **thermosphere**, 50-280 miles (80-450 km). Increased height adds significantly to the temperature, which can reach thousands of degrees. The space shuttle orbits the Earth in this zone.

The **mesosphere**, 30-50 miles (50-80 km). Meteorite showers are seen in this layer of the atmosphere.

The **stratosphere**. Most long-distance aircraft cruise in this layer, and ozone is found here. It extends up to 30 miles (50 km) high.

The **troposphere**. This extends from sea level to about 8 miles (12 km).

Sea level. This is the height at which most life on Earth exists.

OXYGEN AND WATER

Oxygen is the most common element on Earth. It makes up nearly 50% by weight of all the rocks and 89% by weight of all water. Oxygen is constantly being used and replaced in what is called the Oxygen Cycle: animals breathe oxygen in and exhale carbon dioxide, while plants absorb carbon dioxide and "exhale" oxygen. It combines with another gas, hydrogen, to form water, one of the basic necessities for life on Earth.

Volcanic eruptions use up oxygen.

Photosynthesis produces oxygen.

Oxygen in rain

Animals breathe in oxygen during respiration.

Photosynthesis by marine plants produces oxygen.

The Oxygen Cycle

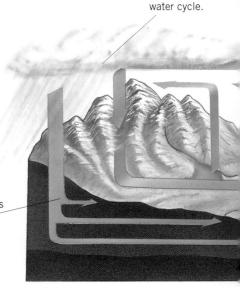

Rain and snow put water back into the water cycle.

Water seeps into the soil and eventually returns to the sea.

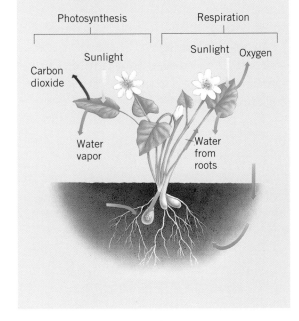

PHOTOSYNTHESIS

Plants and trees produce oxygen by a process called photosynthesis (shown below). Carbon dioxide is absorbed from the air and from soil, and is combined with sunlight to make sugars – their food. Oxygen is then "exhaled." Plants release energy from sugars by a process called respiration, in which oxygen and water vapor are given off as by-products.

Photosynthesis | Respiration

Sunlight

Carbon dioxide

Sunlight Oxygen

Water vapor

Water from roots

◄ *The Earth's atmosphere – the air – helps block out harmful rays from the Sun. Air is made up of 78% nitrogen, 21% oxygen, and traces of other gases.*

The discovery of oxygen

Joseph Priestley lived in Leeds, England. He traveled to London to attend meetings of the Royal Society, where scientists discussed their discoveries. He also visited Antoine Lavoisier, who worked in Paris, France.

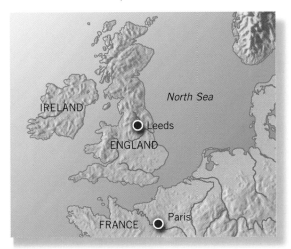

IRELAND

North Sea

Leeds

ENGLAND

Paris

FRANCE

► *Joseph Priestley (1733-1804) was the son of a cloth worker. He taught himself about science by reading and by doing his own experiments.*

▼ *Antoine Lavoisier (1743-1794) demonstrates to his colleagues his discovery that air is a mixture of gases.*

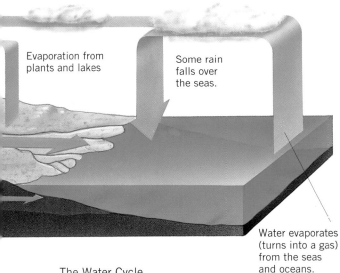

Clouds form when water cools and condenses.

Evaporation from plants and lakes

Some rain falls over the seas.

Water evaporates (turns into a gas) from the seas and oceans.

The Water Cycle

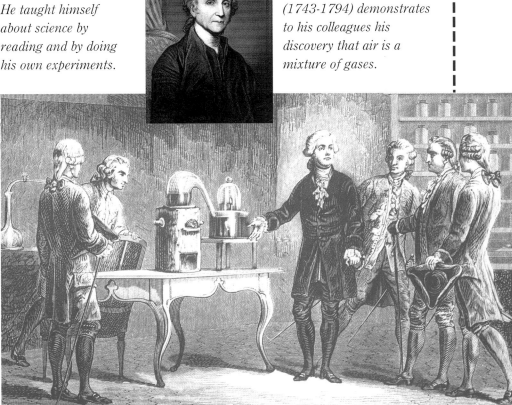

Plastics

PLASTICS HAVE TRANSFORMED the world. They have replaced metals, wood, glass, and even stone for many purposes. They are light, easily shaped, and can be made in any color. They do not rust or corrode, and many hundreds of different kinds can now be made, each with distinct properties.

Plastic is made by forming long chains of small molecules into larger molecules called polymers (from the Greek word for "many parts").

There are two different types of plastic: thermoplastics and thermosetting plastics. When thermoplastics are heated, the molecules move across each other. The plastic softens so that it can be shaped and molded. When it cools it retains its shape, but if it is reheated it will soften again and can be reshaped. Polythene, Perspex, and PVC (polyvinyl chloride) are examples of thermoplastics.

Thermosetting plastics, which have a network of interlinked chains, set hard on heating and will not soften again if reheated. The first thermosetting plastic, Bakelite, was invented in 1909. It was used to make telephones and cameras because it is very hard.

In the 1930s, British scientists made polythene (polyethene or polyethylene) from petroleum oil. Almost all plastics are now made from oil or natural gas.

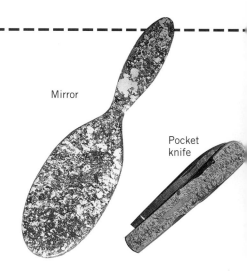

Mirror

Pocket knife

▶ *This mirror and pocket knife are made from Parkesine, a crude early form of plastic invented by an English chemist, Alexander Parkes, in 1855. He made it from cellulose (a chain of sugar molecules), nitric acid, alcohol, and vegetable oil.*

Early plastic manufacture

The first plastic, celluloid, was made from cotton and camphor by John Hyatt in New York in 1871. The first artificial clothing fiber, viscose rayon, was made by Charles Cross in Brentford, England, in 1892.

NORTH AMERICA

New York

Atlantic Ocean

ORGANIC MATERIALS

Plastics are organic ("to do with life") materials because they are composed of the element carbon, which is the basic building block of all living things. Carbon is the only element that can join onto itself to form long chains of molecules, like bead necklaces. Molecules are groups of atoms. A water molecule, for example, is two hydrogen atoms bonded to one oxygen atom.

Carbon atom

Hydrogen atom

◀ *At this scale (magnified thousands of times), a piece of polythene molecule like this would stretch for more than 3,300 feet (1,000 meters).*

▼ *Hundreds of different plastics can now be made, each with its own distinct properties – hard or soft, firm or flexible.*

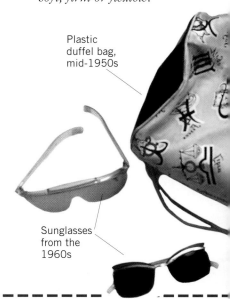

Plastic duffel bag, mid-1950s

Sunglasses from the 1960s

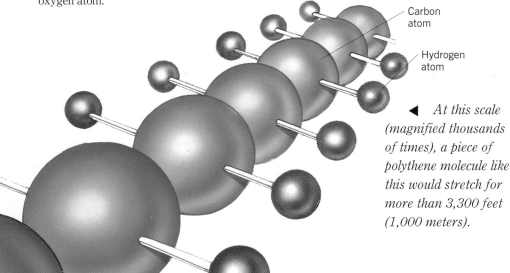

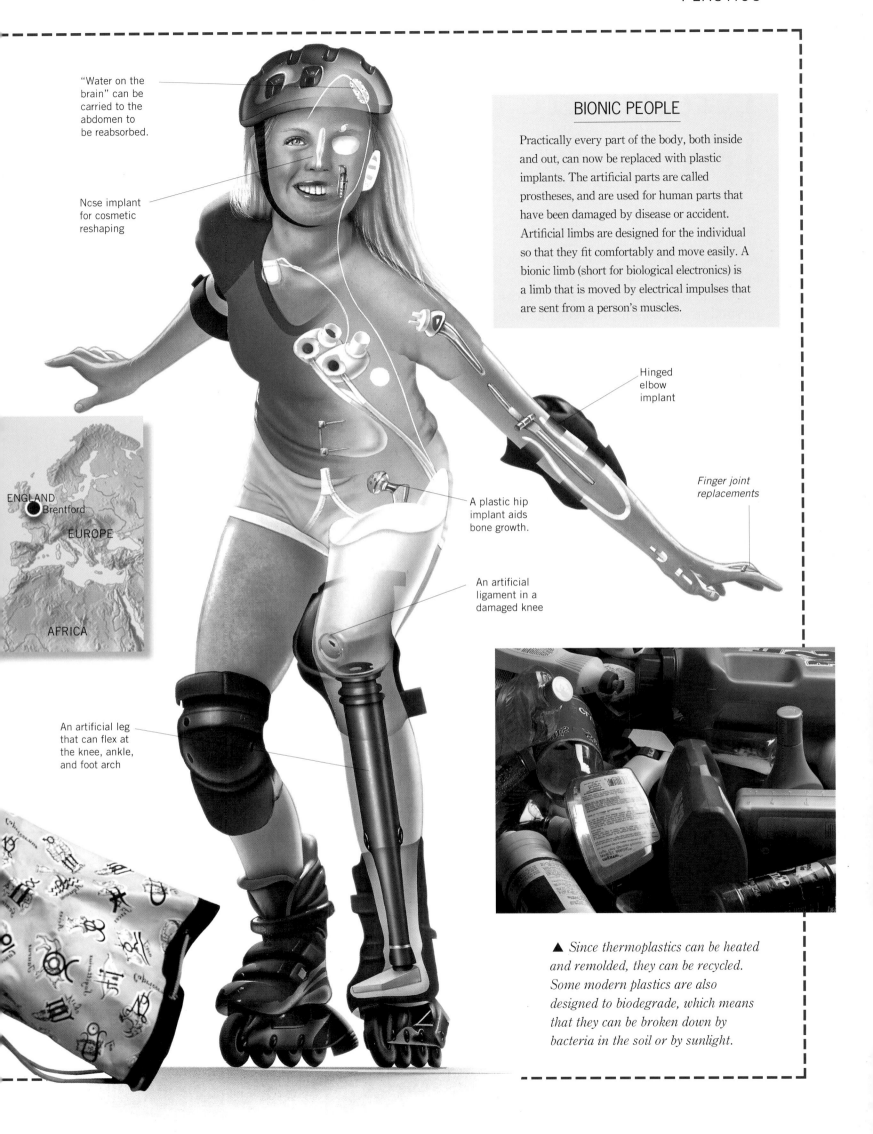

"Water on the brain" can be carried to the abdomen to be reabsorbed.

Ncse implant for cosmetic reshaping

BIONIC PEOPLE

Practically every part of the body, both inside and out, can now be replaced with plastic implants. The artificial parts are called prostheses, and are used for human parts that have been damaged by disease or accident. Artificial limbs are designed for the individual so that they fit comfortably and move easily. A bionic limb (short for biological electronics) is a limb that is moved by electrical impulses that are sent from a person's muscles.

Hinged elbow implant

Finger joint replacements

ENGLAND
Brentford

EUROPE

AFRICA

A plastic hip implant aids bone growth.

An artificial ligament in a damaged knee

An artificial leg that can flex at the knee, ankle, and foot arch

▲ *Since thermoplastics can be heated and remolded, they can be recycled. Some modern plastics are also designed to biodegrade, which means that they can be broken down by bacteria in the soil or by sunlight.*

Radioactivity and Invisible Rays

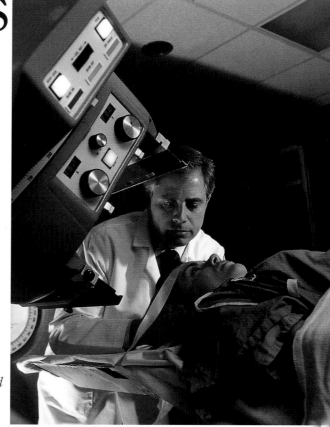

▶ *In radiotherapy, a controlled dose of radiation is used to kill cancerous cells in the body.*

IN 1896, HENRI BECQUEREL, a French physicist, discovered a phenomenon that the Polish scientist Marie Curie later named radioactivity. Radioactivity is a stream of tiny subatomic particles and high-energy rays that are given off by large, unstable atoms as they decay and become more stable atoms. Radiation is harmful to living things. There are three forms of radiation: alpha, beta, and gamma rays. Alpha rays, made up of two protons and two neutrons, are the weakest; they travel at 10 percent the speed of light and cannot pass through a sheet of paper. Beta rays are electrons that travel at half the speed of light and can pass through paper but not metal. Gamma rays, like X-rays, are very high-energy electromagnetic waves or photons. They travel at the speed of light and can be stopped only by thick lead or concrete.

Radiation has some important uses, including radiotherapy, where measured doses are used to kill cancer cells and stop them spreading.

X-RAYS

X-rays form part of the spectrum of invisible light rays *(see* page 23). They are not as penetrating as gamma rays but have enough energy to pass through some materials, including skin, but not bone, which is denser. Because of this, X-rays are used to look inside the body for damaged bones or teeth.

X-rays were discovered in 1895 by a German physicist, Wilhelm Roentgen, when he was using a cathode ray tube, which is a machine for producing a very narrow beam of electrons. When this beam hit a piece of fluorescent paper placed at the end of the tube, a spot glowed brightly. Roentgen called this new form of radiation X-rays – X for mystery!

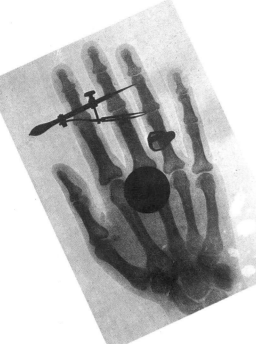

▲ *Wilhelm Roentgen took this early X-ray of his wife's hand in 1895.*

▶ *X-rays are a form of radiation, so they can damage living cells. Because of this, they are used in controlled doses and in a sealed environment.*

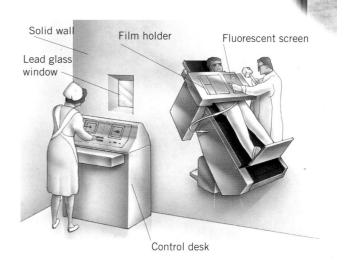

Solid wall

Film holder

Fluorescent screen

Lead glass window

Control desk

Where radiation was studied

Wilhelm Roentgen discovered X-rays in the laboratories of Würzburg University in Germany. Marie Curie was from Warsaw, Poland, but studied radioactivity in Paris.

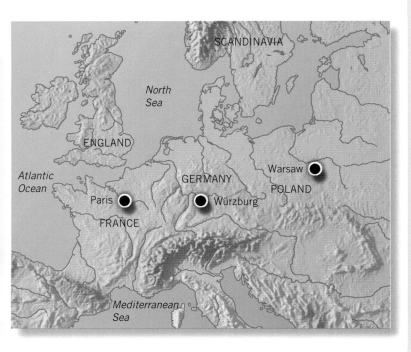

BODY SCANNERS

Thin beams of X-rays are used to examine sections of a patient's body from different angles to identify possible injury. The results are fed into a computer, which produces a detailed internal view of that section. The scientific term for this technique is computerized tomography (CT).

▲ *A patient is slid into a CT scanner while a technician views the computerized scan from a sealed room.*

▼ *This CT scan shows a section through the spine, kidneys, and intestines of a patient.*

▲ *The Polish scientist Marie Curie in her laboratory. Her most influential work, with her husband Pierre, was in finding out which elements are radioactive. In doing so, she discovered two new elements – radium and polonium.*

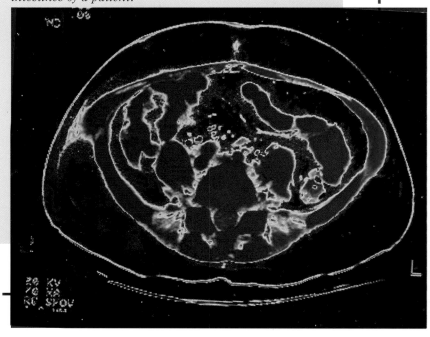

Moving Continents

▶ *Mountains are formed when two plates converge, forcing the continental material upward.*

LOOK AT A MAP OF THE CONTINENTS. What would happen if you moved them around a bit? Does anything strike you?

In 1620, the English philosopher and scientist Francis Bacon noticed that the eastern coast of South America and the western coast of Africa seemed to fit together, and thought it couldn't be an accident. But the ocean floors are made of rock. How could they move?

Evidence for the movement of continents – called continental drift – came in the 1950s. When rocks are formed, they carry a slight magnetic charge according to the direction they lie in the Earth's magnetic field (*see* pages 20-21). A team of British and Japanese geologists noticed that the magnetism in rocks of various ages lies in different directions. The magnetic north pole moves only marginally, so the continents themselves must have wandered.

In 1967, American Jason Morgan brought all the evidence together in a theory called plate tectonics. It suggests that continents and ocean floors lie on larger rocky plates 30-60 miles (50-100 km) thick, which are broken up like a cracked eggshell. These plates slide slowly over a denser layer of rock below, called the mantle. When plates collide, earthquakes can occur, and they can push up new mountain ranges.

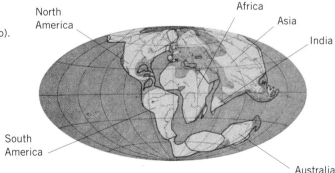

Pangea existed about 200 million years ago, during the Carboniferous period (345-280 million years ago).

CONTINENTAL DRIFT

In 1912, German astronomer and meteorologist Alfred Wegener published his theory of continental drift. He suggested that millions of years ago there had been just one landmass (which he called Pangea, meaning "all land") on the face of the Earth. This split up, forming continental masses, which drifted over millions of years into the positions they are in today. These illustrations, from Alfred Wegener's article, show three stages of continental drift.

During the Eocene period (60-30 million years ago), South America and Africa split and the Atlantic Ocean was formed. India also moved northward. Modern life forms began to evolve after the death of the dinosaurs.

Earth's continental plates

There are six major plates that form the face of the earth (American, Eurasian, African, Indo-Australian, Pacific, and Antarctic). Smaller plates, such as the Arabian and Caribbean plates, fit in between. The arrow heads indicate where plates are moving apart (in the middle of oceans), and where they are pushing together (mostly at the edges of continents).

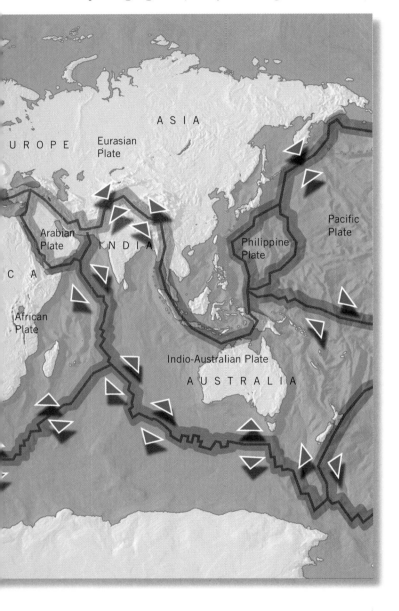

▲ *Melted rock called magma rises from deep within the Earth and erupts as lava. This erupting volcano is on Reunion Island in the Indian Ocean.*

OCEAN FLOOR SPREADING

Where two plates meet in the middle of the ocean, hot molten rock from deep within the Earth, called magma, is forced upward through the gap between them. This new rock pushes the plates apart, causing the sea floor to spread. The opposite edges of oceanic plates slide into and under denser continental plates, causing deep oceanic ridges.

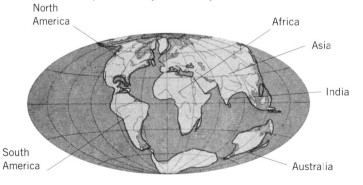

At the start of the Quaternary period (2 million years ago), humans began to evolve. The continents reached the positions they are in today.

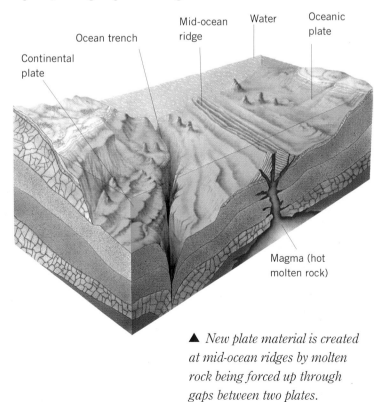

▲ *New plate material is created at mid-ocean ridges by molten rock being forced up through gaps between two plates.*

The Laser

TODAY, LASERS ARE COMMONPLACE. They "read" bar codes on products, and the sound and pictures on compact discs, video discs, and CD-ROMs. They are used in surgery, in engineering, and on battlefields, where they are used to aim missiles. But what are they?

The word "laser" stands for Light Amplification by the Stimulated Emission of Radiation. Just as sound amplifiers make sounds louder, lasers amplify light, making it brighter. This is achieved by forcing light waves, which usually travel in a loose way across a wide area, to travel very neatly in the same direction.

Lasers work on a principle discovered in 1917 by Albert Einstein and others. When atoms absorb photons of light (energy), they become "excited" (meaning they have a high level of energy). If they are then hit by other photons, extra bursts of light energy are released but they all travel in exactly the same direction. This is what "the stimulated emission of radiation" means, because light is a form of radiation.

In the 1950s, the American Charles Townes invented the maser, which produces an intense beam of energy in the form of microwaves. However, the first real, visible light laser was made by Theodore Maiman in 1960 in the United States. He used a bar of artificial ruby to produce the most powerful light ever seen except from a star.

LASER BEAMS

Inside a laser, light from an external source is trapped between partially silvered mirrors. The atoms of a crystal or gas absorb particles of light (photons) and become excited. The atoms release energy in the form of light, stimulating more atoms. The light becomes intense as it is reflected back and forth, and emerges as a powerful beam.

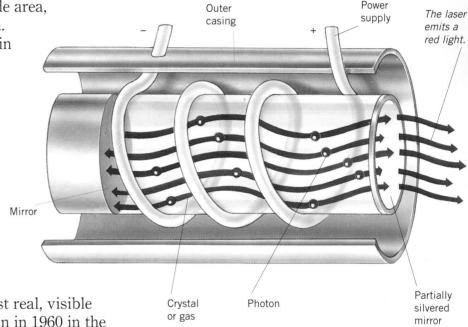

Outer casing

Power supply

The laser emits a red light.

Mirror

Crystal or gas

Photon

Partially silvered mirror

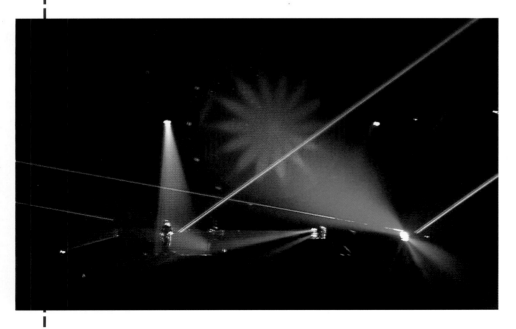

◀ *Lasers are used to paint sky pictures at firework displays and rock concerts, like this one by the English rock group Pink Floyd.*

Berkeley

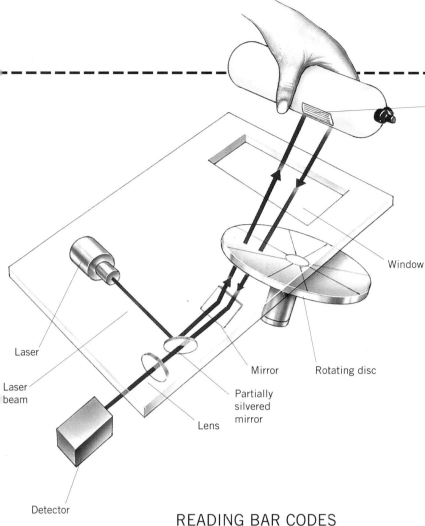

A bar code is a pattern of stripes that encode information.

Window

Laser

Laser beam

Mirror

Rotating disc

Partially silvered mirror

Lens

Detector

Number system

5 or 6 digit manufacturer's number

5 or 6 digit product number assigned by manufacturer

Check digit

READING BAR CODES

Lasers are used in stores to read bar codes. When an item is sold, the laser at the checkout reads the bar code and records the price and other information in the register and on the receipt. This information is also passed on to a central database for monitoring stock levels.

Inventors at work

Einstein was based in Zurich, Switzerland. Charles Townes worked on the maser in Greenville, South Carolina and Berkeley, California.

▲ *Engineers working on the Channel Tunnel between England and France used lasers to guide the tunneling equipment on a straight path.*

▶ *Lasers have many uses in medicine. Here lasers in an endoscope enable the surgeon to see inside the patient's body.*

EUROPE

Zurich

NORTH AMERICA

Greenville

Atlantic Ocean

AFRICA

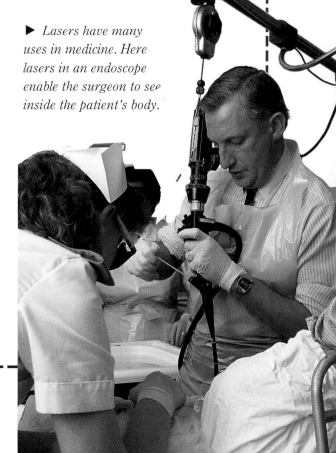

Nuclear Power

T HE POWER OF THE ATOMIC NUCLEUS is one of the most useful discoveries of the 20th century – but also one of the most frightening.

In 1939, Otto Hahn and Fritz Strassman discovered nuclear fission. This occurs when a neutron hits the nucleus of a heavy radioactive atom, like uranium, and splits it in half, releasing a massive amount of energy (much more than burning a fuel ever does).

In Chicago in 1942, Italian physicist Enrico Fermi demonstrated that fission produces a chain reaction – when a nucleus splits, it releases subatomic particles that hit other nuclei and cause them to split as well. He made the first nuclear reactor in an old squash court at the University of Chicago. Fermi and his colleagues watched the world's first nuclear chain reaction take place in awed silence – the Nuclear Age was born.

▲ *Professor Fermi set up the first nuclear chain reaction. In Fermi's experiment, six tons of pure uranium was caused to react inside 1,400 tons of black graphite bricks in a disused squash court. The graphite was used to contain the nuclear reaction.*

NUCLEAR REACTORS

Nuclear reactors are power stations that produce energy from nuclear reactions. Heat is generated by fuel rods of uranium, which are covered by a material called a moderator, which controls the rate of the nuclear reaction. The heat converts water into steam, which is then used to generate electricity. The fuel rods have to be stored securely once they have been used up because they remain radioactive for thousands of years.

▶ *Nuclear power stations produce millions of times more electricity than coal can produce from the same amount of fuel.*

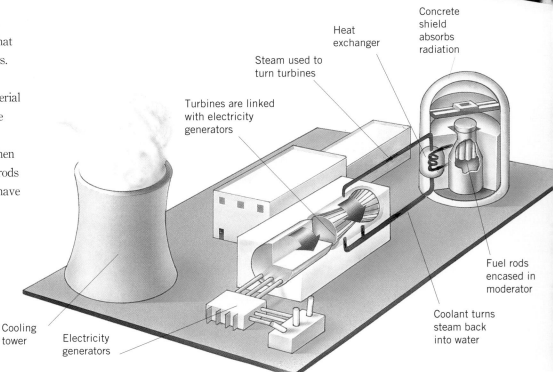

Heat exchanger

Concrete shield absorbs radiation

Steam used to turn turbines

Turbines are linked with electricity generators

Fuel rods encased in moderator

Coolant turns steam back into water

Cooling tower

Electricity generators

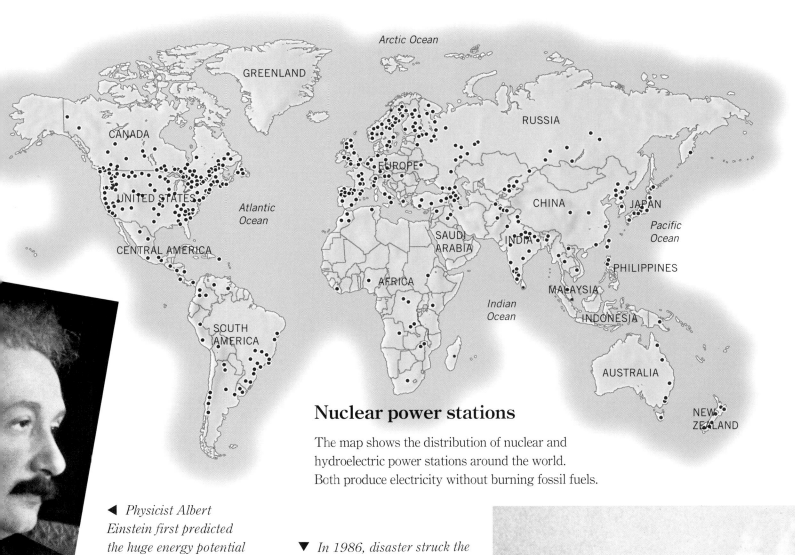

Nuclear power stations

The map shows the distribution of nuclear and hydroelectric power stations around the world. Both produce electricity without burning fossil fuels.

◀ *Physicist Albert Einstein first predicted the huge energy potential of the atomic nucleus in the first decade of the 20th century.*

▼ *In 1986, disaster struck the Chernobyl Nuclear Power Station in the Ukraine. The core overheated and exploded, sending radioactive material into the air.*

▲ *The devastationg power of nuclear fission was first seen in 1945 when the atomic bomb was tested – six years before the first nuclear power station was built.*

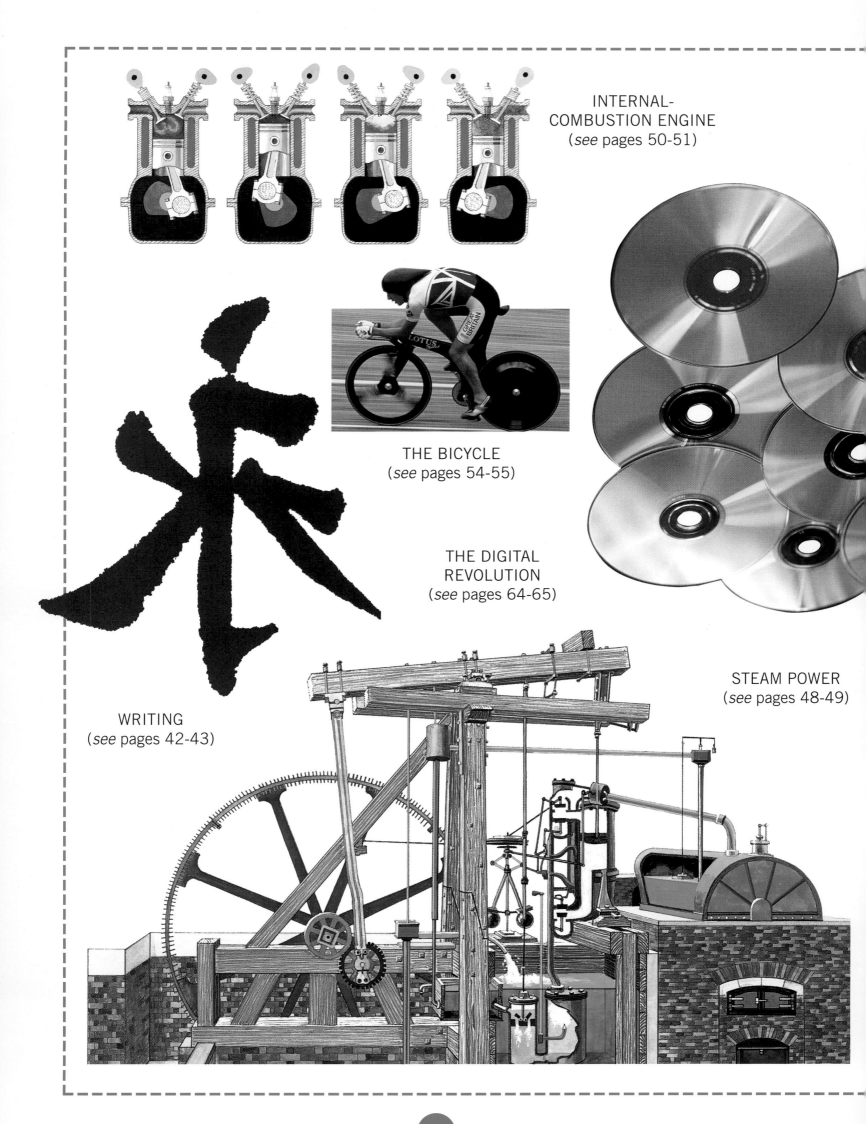

INTERNAL-
COMBUSTION ENGINE
(*see* pages 50-51)

THE BICYCLE
(*see* pages 54-55)

THE DIGITAL
REVOLUTION
(*see* pages 64-65)

STEAM POWER
(*see* pages 48-49)

WRITING
(*see* pages 42-43)

COMMUNICATIONS AND TRAVEL

Early in history, people began to record ideas in pictures and then in written words. Writing preserved orders, laws, ideas, stories, records, and discoveries for future generations.

Five hundred years ago, printing brought a revolution in communication. Printed books were easier to produce, so ideas and knowledge spread faster.

All the same, a message could travel only as fast as a person could carry it. Water transport improved with the advent of sails and better navigation, but the speed of travel didn't increase much until the mid-19th century. The invention of the steam engine led to the steamship and the railway train, as well as mechanized factories and mills. Advances in transportation also meant people could travel more widely by car, plane, or bicycle.

Electricity dramatically changed communication. The electric telegraph, invented in the 1840s, could carry a message great distances in seconds. The telephone, radio, television, and moving pictures soon followed.

Today, with satellites, mobile phones, and the Internet computer network, we can exchange information with practically anyone anywhere in the world. This section tells how that became possible.

Writing

WRITING PROVIDES A UNIQUE WAY of recording and sharing experiences, ideas, and discoveries. The earliest forms of "writing" were cave paintings and rock drawings made by Stone Age people. The exact meanings of these detailed pictures may never be known.

Ways of recording numbers came before words. Clay tablets were used as counters in the Middle East as long ago as 8000 B.C.

The first real writing appeared in Mesopotamia, the valley between the rivers Tigris and Euphrates in the area where Iraq is now, in about 3300 B.C. The Sumerians, who lived here, scratched pictures on clay tablets, which soon became pictographic symbols (visual representations of objects). Within 200 years, a writing called cuneiform had developed – a system of standardized wedge-shaped marks that still resembled the objects they symbolized.

About 3100 B.C., another system, called hieroglyphic writing, was used in Egypt. Hieroglyphs were also pictographs, but gradually they came to refer to sounds instead of objects.

The first alphabet – a set of symbols representing particular sounds, no matter what the language – appeared sometime before 1600 B.C. in the eastern Mediterranean. The English alphabet used today derives from the Romans, who in turn had developed it from the earlier Greek alphabet.

NORTH AMERICA

CENTRAL AMERICA

Pacific Ocean

▲ *This prehistoric cave painting comes from Libya, in the Middle East. Writing developed from picture words and came to use abstract shapes to make words that could express things or ideas.*

Hieroglyphics

THE ROSETTA STONE

In 1799, during the French general Napoleon's invasion of Egypt, a soldier found a stone tablet in a village called Rosetta. It was inscribed with the same piece of text in three languages: Greek, demotic (a form of Egyptian shorthand), and hieroglyphs. It was the key to understanding Egyptian hieroglyphs, which had been unreadable since the language had disappeared at the end of the ancient Egyptian empire.

◀ *The demotic script ("of the people") on the Rosetta Stone is a more rapidly written (cursive) form of hieroglyphics.*

Demotic script

Greek

Development of writing

Each of the empires shown developed early forms of writing.

- Ancient China (2000 B.C.-700 B.C.)
- Indus Valley (2300 B.C.-1700 B.C.)
- Mesopotamia (3200 B.C.-300 B.C.)
- Ancient Egypt (3100 B.C.-332 B.C.)
- Ancient Greece (1000 B.C.-338 B.C.)
- Ancient Rome (200 B.C.-A.D. 550)
- Mayan Empire (200 B.C.-A.D. 1000)

◄ *Wedge-shaped cuneiform script was used 5,000 years ago in Mesopotamia. Here are a clay legal document, left, and an envelope, below. The earliest known examples of writing were trade agreements or lists of produce.*

▲ *Chinese pictogram writing first appeared in about 1200 B.C. The Chinese and Japanese languages today still use pictograms, with "alphabets" of hundreds of characters.*

▲ *Arabic writing, shown in this page from the* Koran, *is the source for modern numerals. This is partly because Arabic had a symbol for zero, lacking in other written languages.*

Paper and Printing

Paper was originally made in China in about A.D. 105 using a mesh frame dipped into a cooked mixture of mashed tree bark, old rags, and fishing nets. The thin layer of pulp left on the screen after it was lifted out was pressed and dried to form a sheet of paper. Today, machines and chemicals are used to manufacture paper, but the principle remains the same, and most paper is still made from wood or plant materials.

Printing also developed in China. A written page was pressed onto a wooden board, leaving ink on the wood. An engraver then chiseled away the uninked areas so the writing stood out in reverse. This was brushed with ink, and paper was laid on top. In 1450, a German inventor named Johannes Gutenberg revolutionized printing. He made movable letters by casting metal in molds – actually also used in a limited way by the Chinese as early as the 11th century. Metal produced sharper print, and lasted longer than wood or clay. Gutenberg's masterstroke was the printing press, which applied pressure to make the ink print firmly and clearly onto the page.

Printing made it much easier to produce books, which until then had been copied by hand, usually by monks.

▲ *Johannes Gutenberg, who invented the printing press, is shown here examining a page from his first printed book, the* Bible.

EARLY PAPER

Papyrus is a form of writing material used in ancient Egypt 3,500 years before paper was invented. It is made from a plant called papyrus that grew abundantly in the Nile River.

In the Middle Ages, people in Europe wrote on a form of writing surface made from animal skins called parchment.

▶ *Papyrus is a rough-grained paper used by the Ancient Egyptians.*

◀ *A page from the first book ever to be printed, Gutenberg's Latin-language edition of the* Bible, *published in 1456.*

▶ *Modern printing plants, such as those that print daily newspapers, feed through huge reels of paper that is printed on both sides and then cut and folded to make up an eight-page section of a newspaper.*

Papermaking

Papermaking spread from ancient China, where it was first produced in the 2nd century A.D., to Arabia via the important trading center of Samarkand in the 8th century. From there it spread slowly throughout Europe.

◀ *The invention of printing enabled books to be manufactured in large numbers, which rapidly encouraged the demand for knowledge. This engraving shows Gutenberg's first printing press. It works by inking by hand a page of type, laying a paper tray over the top and sliding this under a screw-down press.*

FOUR WAYS OF PRINTING

There are four main ways to print: the first three forms (relief, intaglio, lithographic) are used by magazines and newspapers. The fourth, screen printing, is often used on fabrics and textiles, but can also be used for plastic.

❶ Relief printing uses Gutenberg's original method of printing from inked raised areas of wood or metal.

❷ Intaglio is the opposite of relief: an image is cut into the printing plate and the paper absorbs the ink in the holes.

❸ The litho image is drawn in grease. The page is wetted and inked so that, because grease and water repel, only dry parts retain the ink.

❹ Screen prints use stencils attached to a screen or mesh, over which ink is wiped. The ink is squeezed evenly through the mesh.

Ships and Navigation

THE EARLIEST BOATS WERE HOLLOWED-OUT LOGS and rafts made of reeds and branches. Slowly, as boat builders learned their skills, boats became better shaped for cutting through water. By 2000 B.C. the Egyptians were trading in boats with simple square sails as well as oars.

The Ancient Greeks needed fast, powerful ships for war and for trade. The triremes, built about 2,500 years ago in Athens, were fearsome warships. They carried archers and heavily armed soldiers, and were crewed by 170 oarsmen sitting in three layers. A piper played to keep the rowers in time. With a light pinewood hull, two big rudder paddles at the stern, and an underwater ram jutting out under the bow, a trireme could move and turn quickly, ramming enemy ships to sink them before they could escape.

Cargo boats

The Greeks and later the Romans had good cargo ships too. Roman sail-powered corbitas could carry as much as 400 tons. They sailed all around Europe, and even as far as India.

NAVIGATION

The first people to navigate by the Sun and stars were the Polynesians of the South Pacific. The ancient Chinese invented the magnetic compass, with a magnetized needle, which points north when floating in water. The compass arrived in Europe from China via Arabia in the 11th century. The magnetic compass was a big advance in navigation for European sailors because compasses point north even when clouds cover the sky.

During the 15th and 16th centuries, increased navigation skills and larger ships allowed explorers to cross the Pacific and Atlantic oceans.

▶ *The figure on this ancient Chinese compass stands on a magnetic stone and always points south.*

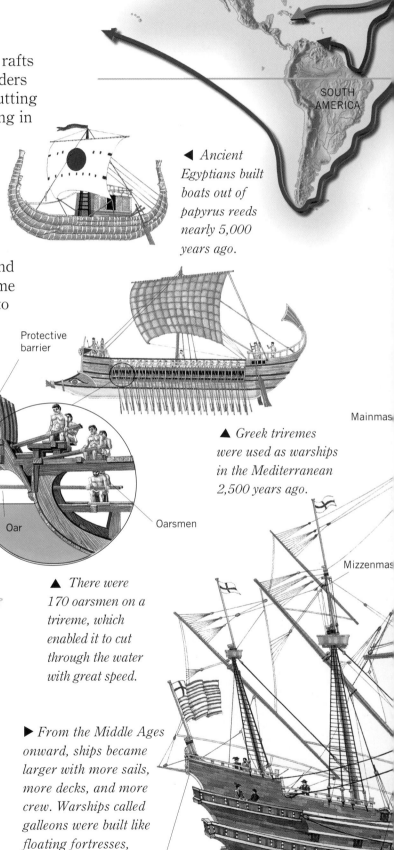

Atlantic Ocean

NORTH AMERICA

SOUTH AMERICA

◀ *Ancient Egyptians built boats out of papyrus reeds nearly 5,000 years ago.*

Protective barrier

Mainmast

▲ *Greek triremes were used as warships in the Mediterranean 2,500 years ago.*

Oar

Oarsmen

▲ *There were 170 oarsmen on a trireme, which enabled it to cut through the water with great speed.*

Mizzenmast

▶ *From the Middle Ages onward, ships became larger with more sails, more decks, and more crew. Warships called galleons were built like floating fortresses, armed with cannon.*

Stern

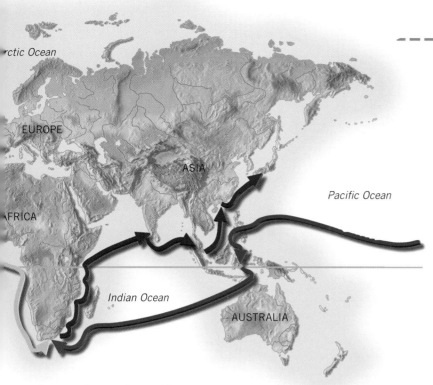

Age of exploration

European sailors in the 15th and 16th centuries traveled to the far corners of the globe in their great ships. The map above shows the routes of some of the most famous of these explorers.

- ☐ Bartolomeu Dias (1487-1488)
- ☐ Christopher Columbus (1492)
- ☐ John Cabot (1497)
- ☐ Vasco da Gama (1497-1499, 1509, 1514, 1543)
- ☐ Amerigo Vespucci (1499-1500)
- ☐ Ferdinand Magellan (1519-1522)

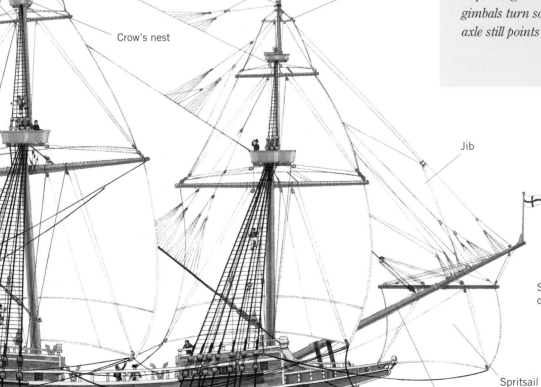

Foremast

Crow's nest

Jib

Spritsail

Bow

Bowsprit

Hull

OCEAN LINERS

Seafaring reached its heyday with the great ocean passenger liners of the early 20th century. These luxury hotels allowed those who could afford it to travel between the continents in style and a comfort unknown to earlier travelers.

▼ *The* United States *is the fastest liner ever. It held the Blue Riband, awarded for the fastest journey across the Atlantic.*

▶ *Gyrocompasses show the direction of north, but are not magnetic. Instead they contain a spinning disc, or rotor, whose axle can be set to point north. The rotor is mounted in frames called gimbals. As the ship changes direction the gimbals turn so that the axle still points north.*

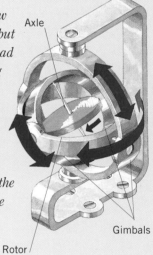

Axle

Gimbals

Rotor

▼ *The Global Positioning System, or GPS, uses satellites to enable seafarers with a suitable receiver to pinpoint their position on the globe to within a few meters.*

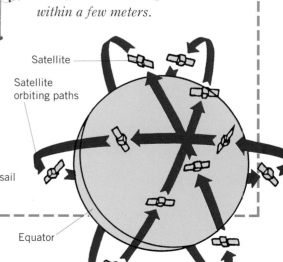

Satellite

Satellite orbiting paths

Equator

Steam Power

For thousands of years, humans relied on their own or their animals' muscle power for work. The Romans harnessed the power of wind and water, but the first real source of modern power was steam.

The earliest steam engines were designed to pump water out of mines. In 1698, an English engineer called Thomas Savery built a contraption known as the Miner's Friend, which used steam to drive air out of a tube. The steam was then cooled by a cold-water spray, causing it to condense (become water), leaving a vacuum. Water from the mineshaft was then forced into this vacuum by outside air pressure. In 1705, a blacksmith, Thomas Newcomen, improved this device by adding a piston in a cylinder. The piston was pushed down by the steam and then sucked up again as the steam condensed and the pressure in the cylinder fell. Both engines were inefficient because in order for them to work, water had to be heated to steam and then cooled again.

In 1769, Scotsman James Watt separated the boiler from the cylinder so that steam could be made continuously. He then linked his machine to a wheel that could run other machines as well as pump water. This development revolutionized industry and transport throughout the world.

▲ *George Stephenson's* Rocket *was the first successful steam locomotive. It set a speed record of 29 mph (47 km/h) in a competition held by the new Liverpool and Manchester Railway in 1829.*

Arrival of steam

The maps above show the extent of the railways in the United States and England in about 1850. These two countries were ahead of the world at the time in the development of the railways. By the mid-19th century, the railway network had revolutionized industry and transport in both countries.

STEAM POWER

Steam was first used as a simple power source hundreds of years before it was reinvented. In about the 1st century A.D., a Greek named Hero made a steam-operated engine called an aeolipile (left) as a toy.

▲ *Hero demonstrating his aeolipile to his colleagues.*

▼ *In James Watt's steam engine, steam passed from the boiler through valves to a separate piston cylinder. It condensed to produce heat energy, which turned the wheel.*

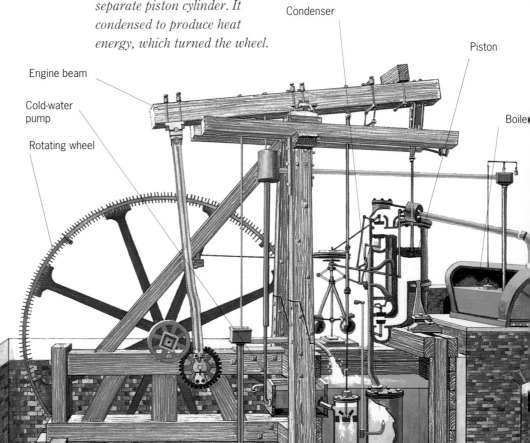

Condenser

Piston

Engine beam

Cold-water pump

Rotating wheel

Boiler

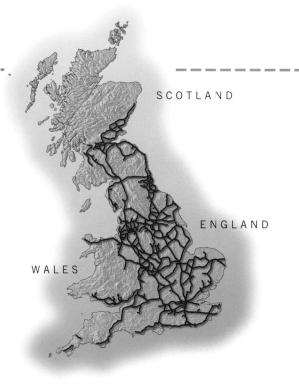

A 4-2-2 engine with a single driving wheel

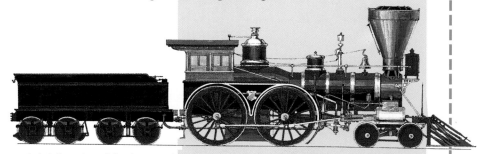

A 4-4-0 engine of the type used in the American West often had a cowcatcher in front to protect the train from obstacles on the track.

Britain's 4-6-2 Mallard *set the world steam speed record of 126 mph (203 km/h) in 1938 (above).*

The Union Pacific 4-8-8-4 "Big Boy" hauled heavy freight in the Rocky Mountains in the 1940s (below).

Trailing   Driving   Driving   Leading

▲ *Engines are identified by the number of leading, driving, and trailing wheels they have.*

STEAM TRAINS

Steam locomotives dominated the world's railway systems in the 19th century. They played an important role in the Industrial Revolution – when machines were first used to do much of the work previously performed by hand – by improving the ease and speed of transport, and in the settlement of new countries, such as the United States and Canada.

▼ *The first steamship was built in America in 1786. By the 1830s, steamships were crossing the Atlantic – and the age of commercial sail was almost over.*

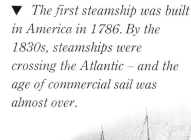

Internal-Combustion Engine

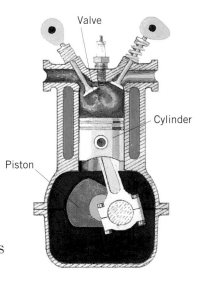
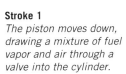

THE STEAM ENGINE WAS A POWERFUL MACHINE, but it was big, noisy, and poorly suited to powering road vehicles. It was the invention of the internal-combustion engine, in which the fuel is burned *inside* the engine rather than *outside*, that made the development of a practical "horseless carriage," or motorcar, possible.

The first workable internal-combustion engine was built by French engineer Etienne Lenoir in 1860. It was a single-cylinder engine, fueled with coal gas. When the gas was burned inside the cylinder, it caused a tiny explosion that pushed the piston down and turned the wheel. Lenoir put his engine on a small carriage in 1862 and made the first-ever journey in a motorcar, traveling 124 miles (200 km) at a rate of 4 mph (6 km/h). Then, in 1876, German engineer Nikolaus Otto developed a "four-stroke" gas engine, in which there were four movements of the piston for every power stroke. It is upon this design that most modern car engines are based.

Stroke 1
The piston moves down, drawing a mixture of fuel vapor and air through a valve into the cylinder.

Stroke 2
The piston moves back up again, compressing the mixture, which is then ignited by a spark.

▲ *Nikolaus Otto's four-stroke engine has been much improved since it was first built in 1876, but the principle remains the same. Only one of the four strokes is powered by the burning fuel, the rest are driven by the the other pistons in the engine or the momentum of the car.*

THE FIRST CAR

The first true car was built in Germany in 1885, by engineer Karl Benz. He developed a single-cylinder engine powered by gasoline – rather than coal gas – which he fitted to a three-wheeler vehicle. This looked more like a motorized tricycle than a car. At first, there were many problems, not the least that Benz drove it into a brick wall during one of its early trials. But Benz soon improved the design, and his cars began to sell. He built his first four-wheel car in 1893.

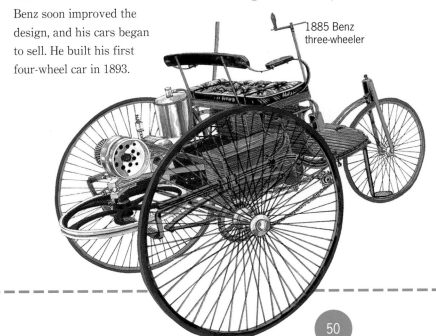

1885 Benz three-wheeler

The rise of Mercedes-Benz

Motoring began in Germany in the 1880s, at the car factories of Karl Benz, in Mannheim, and Gottlieb Daimler, in Cannstatt. Daimler's most successful car was the Mercedes (named for one of the director's daughters), renamed Mercedes-Benz in 1926, when the two firms merged.

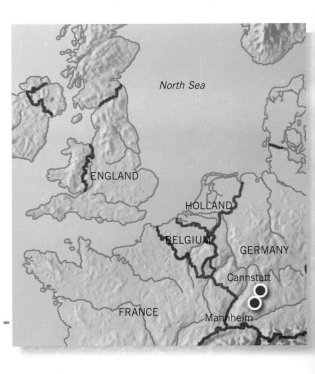

Burnt gases
expellec here

Explosion

Stroke 3
*The resulting
explosion forces
the piston down
on its power
stroke, driving the
engine.*

Stroke 4
*The piston mcves up,
pushing all the burnt
gases out of the
cylinder through a
valve.*

▼ *A modern four-cylinder
internal-combustion engine.
Each piston operates at a
different stage of the four-
stroke cycle, giving a smooth*

*output of power. The valves
are controlled by a camshaft,
and the pistons turn a
crankshaft, which, in turn,
drives the wheels of the car.*

THE FIRST FOUR-WHEEL CAR

In 1885, while Benz was building the first motorcar, two rival
engineers, Gottlieb Daimler and Wilhelm Mayback, were developing
a fast, light, gasoline engine, which they attached to a wooden bicycle
to create the first motorbike. By 1889, Daimler had built the first true
four-wheeled car. Daimler and Benz remained rivals for many years
until their companies were merged in 1926.

◄ *The French firm
Panhard and Levassor
built this four-wheel car
in the 1880s, using a
Daimler gasoline engine.*

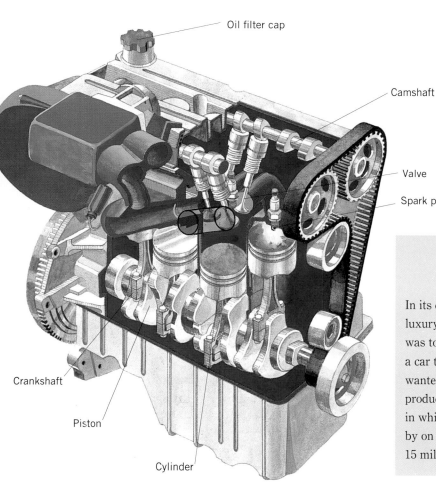

Oil filter cap

Camshaft

Valve

Spark plug

Crankshaft

Piston

Cylinder

CARS FOR THE MASSES

In its early days, the motorcar was an expensive
luxury. But an American named Henry Ford (right)
was to change all that. In 1908 he designed and built
a car that was so cheap and reliable that everyone
wanted to buy one. To reduce costs and speed up
production, Ford developed a moving assembly line
in which workers added various parts to the cars as they passed
by on a huge moving belt. By 1927, when production ceased,
15 million of his Model Ts had rolled off the production line.

Powered Flight

By THE EARLY 20TH CENTURY, people had been flying gliders for several years with some success, though there had also been many disasters. None had succeeded in making a successful flight in a powered aircraft. Then on December 17, 1903, at Kitty Hawk, North Carolina, Orville Wright flew the biplane he had designed and built with his brother Wilbur for 12 seconds, over a distance of 120 feet (37 meters). Later that day Wilbur kept the plane aloft for a staggering 59 seconds! These first-ever powered flights led to a revolution in transport that has given rise to the Jet Age and supersonic aircraft.

Rapid progress in aviation

By 1908 the Wrights had carried the first aircraft passenger, Wilbur had flown 77 miles (124 km) in 160 minutes, and the U.S. Army had taken delivery of the world's first military aircraft. World War I brought major developments in airplanes and flying skills, which greatly advanced postwar aviation. In 1919, John Alcock and Arthur Brown became the first to fly nonstop across the Atlantic. That same year saw the first regular passenger services, using converted bombers. Soon, people were flying across continents and over the poles, and journeys that used to take weeks took only a matter of hours.

The dawn of the Jet Age was heralded in 1937 with the invention of the jet engine by British engineer Frank Whittle. By 1952, the first passenger jet, the *Comet,* had come into service.

Transatlantic flight firsts

In 1919, RAF pilots Alcock and Brown crossed the Atlantic in a Vickers Vimy bomber, flying from Newfoundland to Ireland in 16 hours and 27 minutes. American Charles Lindbergh became a national hero when he made the first solo crossing in 1927, flying his plane, *The Spirit of St. Louis,* from New York to Paris in 33 hours.

CROSSING THE CHANNEL

Inspired by the Wright brothers' success, Frenchman Louis Blériot built a monoplane (an aircraft with a single pair of wings) with a three-cylinder motorcycle engine. On July 25, 1909, he made the first flight across the English Channel, flying his plane from Baraques (near Calais) to Dover in only 37 minutes. This illustration from a French journal of the period shows Blériot arriving in England, over the cliffs of Dover.

▲ *Airplane pioneers Orville and Wilbur Wright owned a bicycle repair shop. In their first aircraft,* Flyer I, *they connected the two propellers to the lightweight gas engine using bicycle chains!*

◄ *In 1930, British aviator Amy Johnson became the first woman to fly solo from Britain to Australia.*

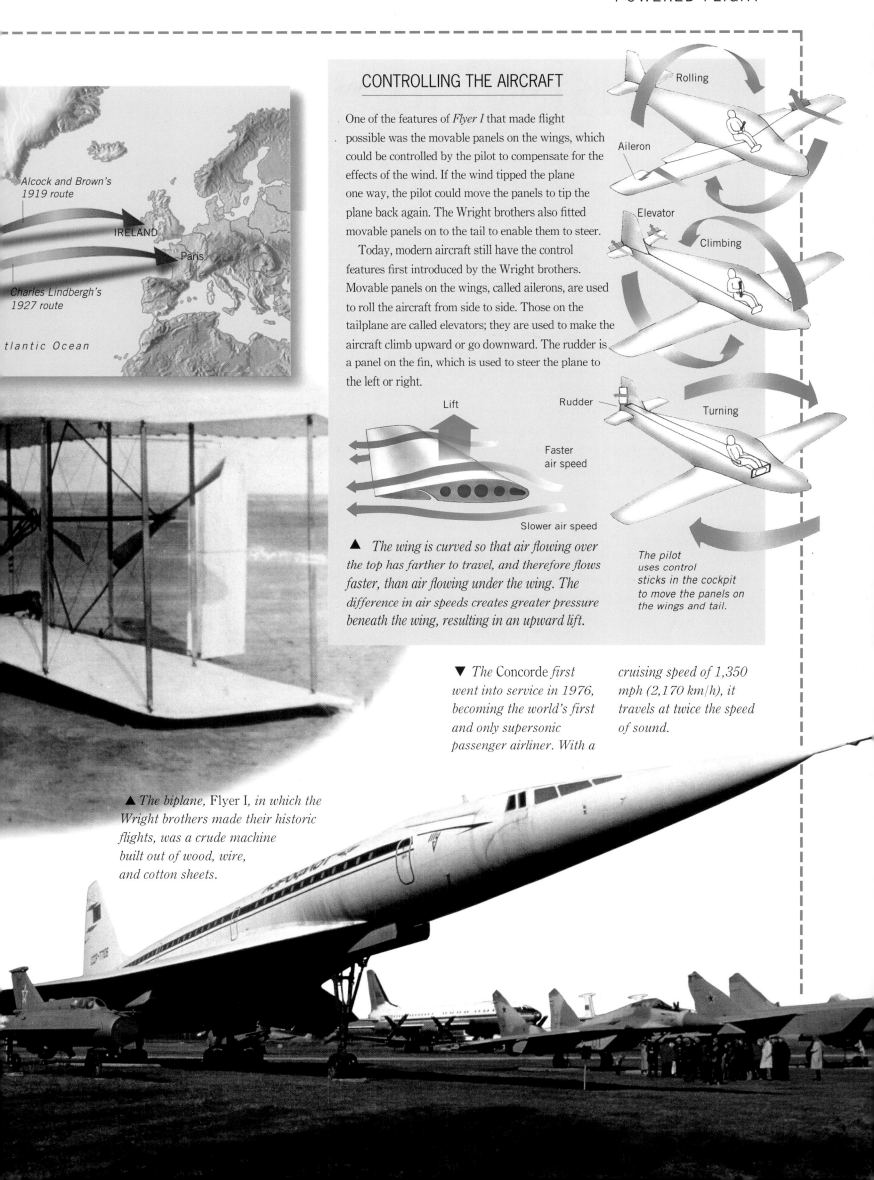

Alcock and Brown's
1919 route

IRELAND

Paris

Charles Lindbergh's
1927 route

tlantic Ocean

CONTROLLING THE AIRCRAFT

One of the features of *Flyer I* that made flight possible was the movable panels on the wings, which could be controlled by the pilot to compensate for the effects of the wind. If the wind tipped the plane one way, the pilot could move the panels to tip the plane back again. The Wright brothers also fitted movable panels on to the tail to enable them to steer.

Today, modern aircraft still have the control features first introduced by the Wright brothers. Movable panels on the wings, called ailerons, are used to roll the aircraft from side to side. Those on the tailplane are called elevators; they are used to make the aircraft climb upward or go downward. The rudder is a panel on the fin, which is used to steer the plane to the left or right.

Rolling

Aileron

Elevator

Climbing

Lift

Rudder

Turning

Faster
air speed

Slower air speed

▲ *The wing is curved so that air flowing over the top has farther to travel, and therefore flows faster, than air flowing under the wing. The difference in air speeds creates greater pressure beneath the wing, resulting in an upward lift.*

The pilot uses control sticks in the cockpit to move the panels on the wings and tail.

▼ *The* Concorde *first went into service in 1976, becoming the world's first and only supersonic passenger airliner. With a* *cruising speed of 1,350 mph (2,170 km/h), it travels at twice the speed of sound.*

▲ *The biplane,* Flyer I, *in which the Wright brothers made their historic flights, was a crude machine built out of wood, wire, and cotton sheets.*

The Bicycle

THE BICYCLE WAS INVENTED LESS than 200 years ago. It may puzzle anyone who has ridden a bicycle that nobody thought of it earlier. The bicycle is said to be the most efficient way yet invented of turning human muscle power into movement. It is an important means of transport worldwide. In many countries there are more bicycles than any other kind of vehicle. Cycling is also cheap, healthy, and causes no pollution.

The first two-wheelers

The first two-wheeled "bicycle" was invented in France in 1818 by Baron Karl de Drais de Sauerbrun. It had no pedals or chain. It was made of wood, and the riders balanced on it and just pushed on the road with their feet.

Scottish blacksmith Kirkpatrick Macmillan spent four years developing his more bicycle-like "hobby-horse," and produced it in 1839. Its wheels had iron rims, and it was propelled by two swinging cranks at the front, connected to the back wheel by rods. Pushing the cranks back and forth turned the wheel.

The popularity of the bicycle meant that advances came quickly. The introduction of gears, a chain, brakes, and better design ensured its continuing popularity. It is estimated that more than 800 milion bicycles are in use today.

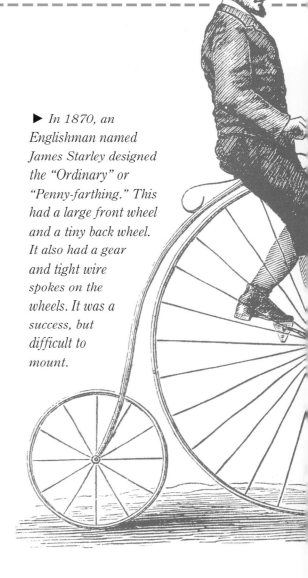

▶ *In 1870, an Englishman named James Starley designed the "Ordinary" or "Penny-farthing." This had a large front wheel and a tiny back wheel. It also had a gear and tight wire spokes on the wheels. It was a success, but difficult to mount.*

THE FIRST POPULAR BICYCLE

After the hobby-horse, many different machines were tried, but nothing exciting happened until 1861, when Pierre Michaux and his son Ernest made their "vélocipède," better known as the bone-shaker because it was so bumpy to ride. It was made of an iron frame with wooden iron-rimmed wheels. It was propelled by cranks, rather like pedals, attached directly to the front wheel. It became popular in the 1860s and 1870s.

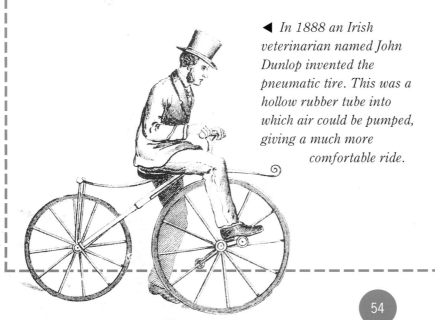

◀ *In 1888 an Irish veterinarian named John Dunlop invented the pneumatic tire. This was a hollow rubber tube into which air could be pumped, giving a much more comfortable ride.*

The Tour de France

France is home to the Tour de France, a cycle race. The race is in stages, with most stages taking a day to complete. Some stages are time trials where the cyclists race against the clock.

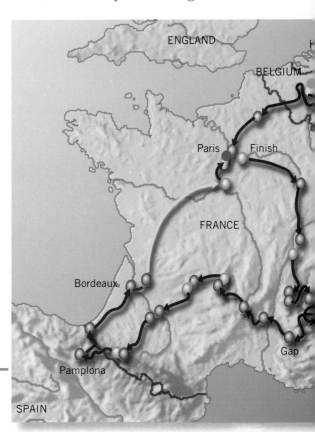

▶ *By the 1890s, the bicycle had become popular throughout Europe and America, as this photograph of the period clearly shows.*

◀ *By 1874, the first "safety" bicycle had been built – so called because the cyclist's feet could touch the ground. This example is the Singer Special, dating from 1886. It is driven by a chain linked to the back wheel.*

KEY

━ Stage

     Transfer by train

━ Time trial

▼ *British cyclist Chris Boardman held the world record for distance covered in one hour. His bicycle was a high-tech machine, specially designed for maximum aerodynamic performance.*

ITALY

Telegraph and Telephone

▲ *Alexander Graham Bell (1847-1922) made the first telephone transmitter in 1876. The first words uttered into it were "Mr. Watson, come here, I want you."*

IN 1800, A MESSAGE TRAVELED only as fast as a horse could gallop or a boat could sail. It might take weeks for news to reach its destination. By 1900, however, messages could cross the world in minutes.

The first long-distance communications device was the electric telegraph. This was an instrument that sent coded signals along wires. British scientists worked on the idea in the 1830s, but were not successful. The signals became too weak because of electrical resistance, even over short distances. It was the American Joseph Henry who made the breakthrough in 1835. He invented the relay to send a current along many miles of wire. Each relay used the fading current to operate a switch that turned on a new current, in the same pattern as the old one, so the signal was boosted from relay to relay.

The first telephone

Alexander Graham Bell was the first man to actually transmit the human voice, by inventing the telephone in 1876. Bell was born in Scotland, but lived in Boston, where he taught deaf children to speak.

Today, telecommunications has changed our world. Using satellites, fiber optics, and worldwide telephone systems, more messages can be sent instantaneously than ever before. The information revolution has happened.

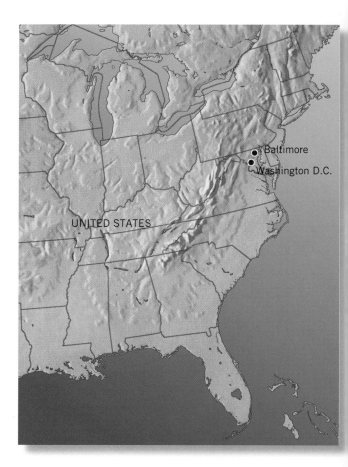

A	• —	M	— —	Y	— • — —
B	— • • •	N	— •	Z	— — • •
C	— • — •	O	— — —	1	• — — — —
D	— • •	P	• — — •	2	• • — — —
E	•	Q	— — • —	3	• • • — —
F	• • — •	R	• — •	4	• • • • —
G	— — •	S	• • •	5	• • • • •
H	• • • •	T	—	6	— • • • •
I	• •	U	• • —	7	— — • • •
J	• — — —	V	• • • —	8	— — — • •
K	— • —	W	• — —	9	— — — — •
L	• — • •	X	— • • —	0	— — — — —

THE MORSE CODE

An American named Samuel Morse (1791-1872) produced the first workable electric telegraph in 1844. He also devised the Morse Code (above). He used the series of dots and dashes to send his messages along the electric telegraph. Within a few years there were telegraph cables across continents and oceans.

Morse's message

In 1844, the year he built the first working telegraph, Samuel Morse sent a famous message from Washington, D.C., to Baltimore. The message, in Morse Code, read "What hath God wrought?"

▶ *Thomas Edison was one of the greatest and most prolific inventors. He worked on and produced the electric light bulb, electric power distribution, the telephone microphone (mouthpiece), and the phonograph. His first invention was the automatic repeater for telegraphic messages, which greatly speeded up sending and receiving messages via the telegraphic system.*

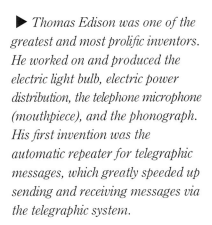

THOMAS EDISON (1847-1931)

The American inventor Edison made the world's first sound recording in 1877 on his phonograph. The words he used were "Mary had a little lamb...." His recording was made by scratching a groove into a wax cylinder. The machine had no electrical parts and relied on mechanical vibrations operating on a needle to both record and replay the sound.

Sound amplifier

Hand crank

Sound recorder

Wax cylinder

Cylinder drive

▲ *Edison's first phonograph was the forerunner of modern sound recording.*

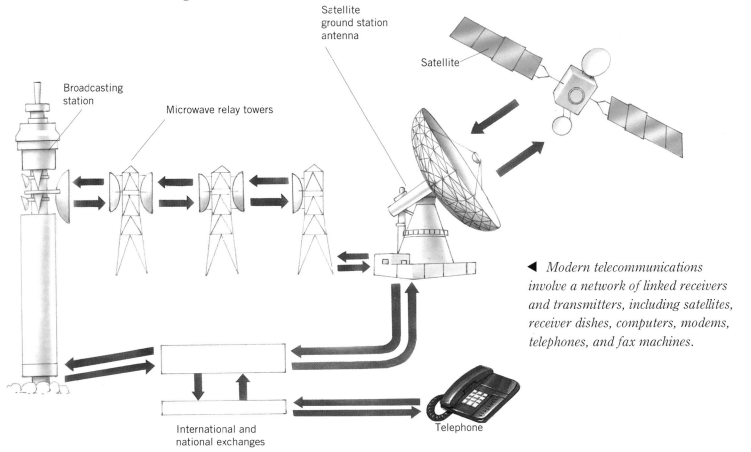

Satellite ground station antenna

Satellite

Broadcasting station

Microwave relay towers

◀ *Modern telecommunications involve a network of linked receivers and transmitters, including satellites, receiver dishes, computers, modems, telephones, and fax machines.*

International and national exchanges

Telephone

Photography and Film

ABOUT 1,000 YEARS AGO, an Arabian scientist noticed that light passing through a tiny hole in one wall would form an upside-down image on the opposite wall of a darkened room. By 1550, this was refined with a lens and a movable screen into the "camera obscura," which is Latin for "dark room" (*see* page 22). However, until the 19th century, the image could not be captured.

In 1839, an English scholar, William Fox Talbot, used a chemical called silver chloride to capture the light. It darkens when light hits it, so parts of a scene that are light become dark, and dark parts remain light. The result is a "negative" image. By reversing the process, he could make any number of "positive" prints from the negative. In 1884, George Eastman in the United States put a chemical gel onto paper, and a few years later onto a new flexible material called celluloid to make photographic film.

By then, people realized that if a number of photographs were taken in quick succession and shown one after another fast enough they would appear to show continuous movement. Two French brothers, Auguste and Louis Lumière, and Thomas Edison in the U.S., pioneered cinema film in the 1890s. Sound was added in the 1920s and color soon after.

◀ *In 1839, Daguerre, shown here in this engraving, took the first photograph of a person.*

▶ *Louis Daguerre designed the first commercially produced camera, based on the "sliding box" that had been used for artists' camera obscuras in the 1700s.*

▼ *William Fox Talbot developed the technique that became the basis of film photography today.*

DAGUERROTYPES

Louis Daguerre was a French theater artist who discovered an early method of fixing an image on a sheet of copper. He found that when a copper sheet is coated with silver and held over a box of iodine, it becomes sensitive to light. The plate has to be held in front of a scene for about twenty minutes. Daguerre then used fumes from hot mercury to "fix" the image and stop it changing any further.

▶ *This is one of Daguerre's photographs (called Daguerrotypes).*

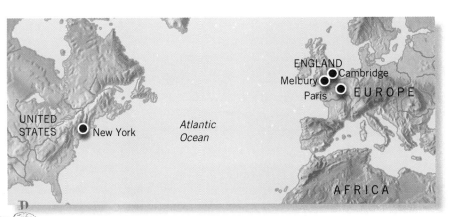

Inventing film

Major advances in photography were made by Daguerre in Paris, France; Fox Talbot in Melbury and Cambridge, England; and Eastman in New York.

▶ *In 1888, George Eastman designed the first Kodak camera, which helped make photography accessible to everyone.*

▲ *Eastman originally produced the Brownie camera for children in 1900. The Brownie name continued to be used for later models until 1982.*

▼ *When the shutter is released by pressing a button, light reflected from the scene is focused onto film. Light entering the lens is controlled by the size of the aperture, or opening.*

▲ *Kodak's No. 2 Bullet camera used the rollfilm (shown on the right) that had recently been introduced. This camera dates from 1895-1900.*

Light rays

Lens

Viewfinder

Aperture

Shutter

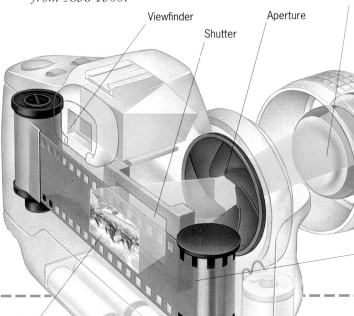

Film cassette

Film image

THE 35MM CAMERA

35mm wide film was first introduced for motion pictures in 1891 and had become a standard by World War I. However, the 35mm camera for still photography wasn't manufactured widely until the 1930s. Today it dominates the industry.

Radio and Television

Radios and televisions are so common in everyday life that it is surprising they have been around for only about 100 years. As long ago as 1863, James Clerk Maxwell, an English physicist, had proved a link between electricity and magnetism (*see* pages 20-21). This led to the discovery of electromagnetic waves. In 1888, a German called Heinrich Hertz, had sent these "radio waves" across a room. Guglielmo Marconi, an Italian engineer, knew of these events and was fascinated by them. In 1895 he used electric sparks to create radio waves that traveled more than a mile (1.5 km). By 1896 he was transmitting signals in Morse Code (*see* page 56) more than 10 miles (15 km). In 1899 he sent a signal across the English Channel, and in 1901 he sent a message across the Atlantic Ocean. Radio technology had arrived.

▲ *Marconi's first radio transmitter and aerial, dating from 1895. He constructed them at his home,* Villa Grifone, *in Italy.*

The first television
When it was found that pictures as well as sound could be transmitted by radio waves, this made television possible. John Logie Baird (1888-1946), a Scottish electrical engineer, was its pioneer. He gave the world's first demonstration of black-and-white television in 1925. The first color television was not introduced until 1953 in the U.S.

THE DIODE VALVE

Until the beginning of the 20th century, radio signals were very weak, and could easily be lost. An English electrical scientist, John Ambrose Fleming (1849-1945), found the solution. In 1904, he invented the diode valve, which could boost a signal. It consists of a glass tube (right) containing gas, which was used to control the flow of electricity in a circuit. This was improved by Lee de Forest (1873-1961), an American physicist who invented the triode valve, used to amplify the electric signal.

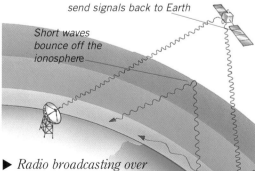

Communications satellite send signals back to Earth

Short waves bounce off the ionosphere

▶ *Radio broadcasting over long distances is achieved by bouncing certain types of radio wave off the upper atmosphere, between 30 and 250 miles (50-400 km) high.*

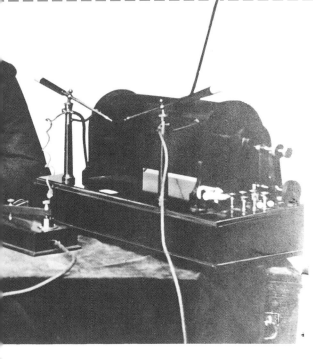

◄ Marconi in 1901, with his transmitting and receiving apparatus that received the first wireless signal across the Atlantic Ocean from Cornwall, England, to Newfoundland.

▲ An early image as it appeared on Baird's televisor.

▲ Baird's first "televisor" could not broadcast sound and pictures together. First, people saw the image of singer Gracie Fields appear on the screen. They heard her sing only after the picture had disappeared.

Origins of radio and television

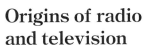

Scottish physicist James Clerk Maxwell came from Edinburgh and worked in Cambridge. Heinrich Hertz was born in Hamburg and worked in Berlin. Guglielmo Marconi came from Bologna and worked in Venice. John Ambrose Fleming worked in Cambridge, while John Logie Baird worked in Glasgow. Physicist Vladimir Zworykin – who patented a color television system as early as 1928 – lived in the U.S. but was born in St. Petersburg.

◄ Television news pictures can be flashed around the world in an instant. In 1963, people worldwide were shocked to see pictures of President Kennedy's assassination on their TV screens.

▶ Inside a TV set is a cathode-ray tube (see page 32). It contains a "gun" that shoots beams of electric particles, called electrons, at the screen. In a color TV there are separate beams for each primary color. On screen the three colors merge to create single color shades.

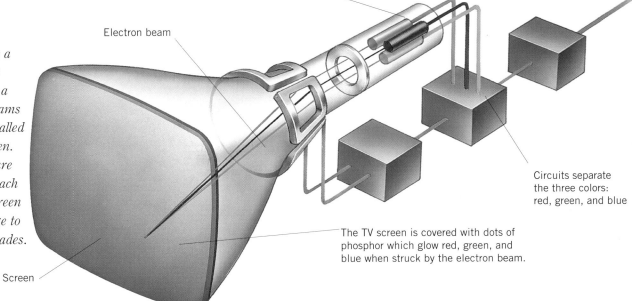

Electron gun

Electron beam

Circuits separate the three colors: red, green, and blue

The TV screen is covered with dots of phosphor which glow red, green, and blue when struck by the electron beam.

Screen

Transistors and the Microchip

ELECTRONICS IS A BRANCH OF SCIENCE AND TECHNOLOGY concerned with the movement of electrons in an electric current (*see* pages 18-19). The electronics industry began in 1904 with the invention of the first electronic component, the diode valve, followed six years later by the invention of the triode valve (*see* page 60). Valves were made of glass, like light bulbs, and broke easily. They were also large and could not be made any smaller, which meant that the devices that used them, such as the first computers (*see* below), had to be large as well.

In 1947, electronics was advanced by the invention of transistors, which perform the same functions as both the diode and the triode valves, but are smaller than either of them. Transistors are made from tiny pieces of material called semiconductors (most commonly silicon), in which an electric current is amplified and flows in one direction only. Electronic equipment, such as the first transistor radio, which appeared in 1954, could now be made much smaller.

In 1958, the first integrated circuit was built combining various electronic components into a single unit. By the 1970s, integrated circuits had been refined to the point where all the components could be etched onto a tiny sliver, or chip, of silicon. These "microchips" are used in microprocessors – the control centers of computers and many of the devices we use every day: washing machines, televisions, video cameras, digital watches, and cars.

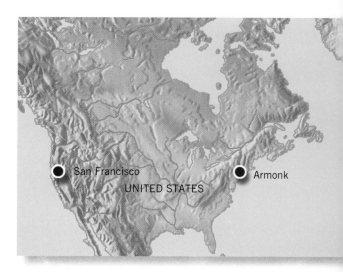

Computer manufacturers

The area around San Francisco is known as Silicon Valley due to the large number of computer firms located here – including Apple. IBM is based in Armonk near New York, and Portsmouth, England. Acorn, an important early firm, is based in Cambridge, England.

◀ *The first portable computers became available in the U.S. in the 1970s. They were bulky and had a fraction of the memory of modern computers.*

THE WORLD'S FIRST COMPUTER

The world's first large electronic computer (called ENIAC, for Electronic Numerical Integrator And Computer) was built in 1946 at the University of Pennsylvania by John Presper Eckert and John Mauchly. It was ordered by the U.S. Army for gunfire calculations. This vast machine contained nearly 19,000 valves, 70,000 resistors (components that resist the flow of an electric current), and 500,000 connections soldered by hand. It weighed 30 tons.

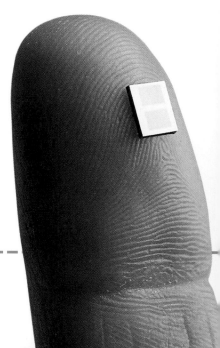

▶ *Although a microchip can contain millions of components, it is smaller than a fingertip.*

▶ *Bill Gates, president of Microsoft, is a leader in the computer revolution that is changing the way people and businesses operate (see page 64).*

▲ *This businessman is using a laptop computer while he travels on an airplane. Computers also reserved his seat, helped design and build the plane, control and monitor the aircraft's systems and flight pattern, and supply the crew with weather reports.*

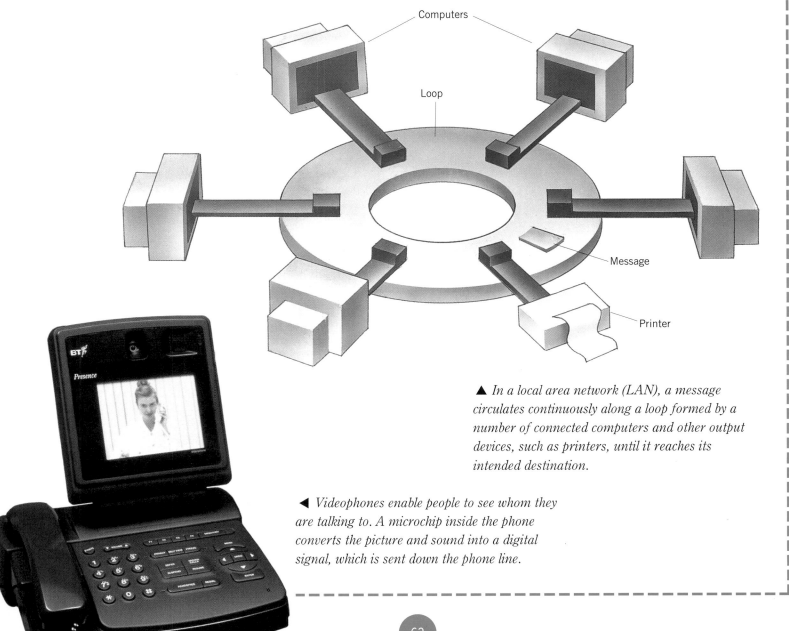

Computers

Loop

Message

Printer

▲ *In a local area network (LAN), a message circulates continuously along a loop formed by a number of connected computers and other output devices, such as printers, until it reaches its intended destination.*

◀ *Videophones enable people to see whom they are talking to. A microchip inside the phone converts the picture and sound into a digital signal, which is sent down the phone line.*

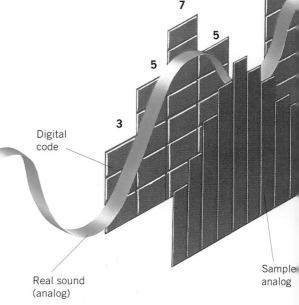

A compact disc

The Digital Revolution

TODAY'S DIGITAL REVOLUTION is a widescale change in the way information is handled and how people (and machines) communicate with each other. The information can be in any form – words, numbers, pictures, speech, music. Information can now be exchanged between people anywhere in the world, almost instantly.

Information is transmitted (sent) using either analog or digital electrical signals. Analog signals are electrical copies of sound or visual signals. They are transmitted in the form of smooth and continuous waves. Digital coverts this "true" sound into a series of pulses that are simply either on or off. On is represented by the number 1 and off by 0. This is called binary code because it uses only two numbers or digits (binary means two).

Digital systems handle information by turning it into a string of 0s and 1s. These numbers are decoded at the receiving end so that the information can be seen again in its original form.

A digital system, such as a computer or a compact disc, has two big advantages: no matter how distorted or faded the digital signal is, the message will get through intact, and it takes up much less space than an analog signal. Until recently the telephone, radio, and television were all analog systems. Now, most telephone calls are transmitted digitally as pulses of light through glass fibers, or using radio or microwave links. This allows room for many more telephone lines. Some television and radio signals are now being broadcast digitally too.

Digital code

Real sound (analog)

Sample analog

▲ *Digital recordings measure the height of sound waves at regular points and give each point a number, which is represented in binary code (combinations of 0 and 1). Sampling is the process by which real sound is stored digitally, but the numbers can be changed to alter the frequency (pitch) of the original sound.*

◀ *Different types of CDs are used to store large amounts of information. There are special CDs for music, photographs (photo CDs), videos (video discs), or computer software or text (CD-ROMs).*

COMPACT DISCS

Music is recorded on a compact disc as a series of etched pits, which represent the on/off numbers in digital code. When a CD is played, a laser scans the pits. As the disc spins at high speed, a detector produces pulses of light according to the on/off pattern of the pits. The electronic circuits in the CD player turn the pulses back into music and send it to the amplifiers and loudspeakers.

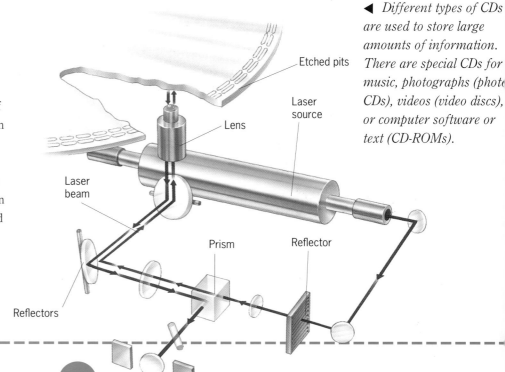

Etched pits

Laser source

Lens

Laser beam

Prism

Reflector

Reflectors

The Information Superhighway

The Internet began in the 1960s as a network of connected computers at U.S. military bases and universities. This map shows a representation of this early network, with several key areas enlarged, and some important sites named.

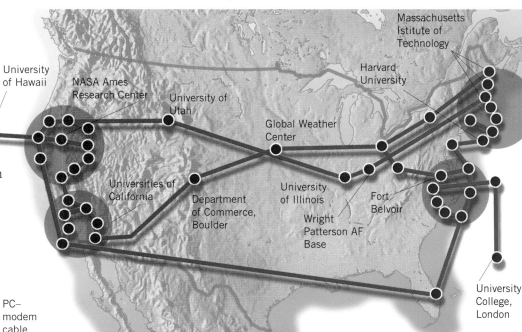

University of Hawaii

NASA Ames Research Center

University of Utah

Massachusetts Istitute of Technology

Harvard University

Global Weather Center

Universities of California

Department of Commerce, Boulder

University of Illinois

Wright Patterson AF Base

Fort Belvoir

University College, London

○ Internet sites

━━━ Network

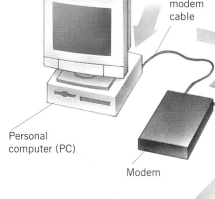

PC–modem cable

Modem–telephone cable

Personal computer (PC)

Modem

Personal computer

Transmission frequencies

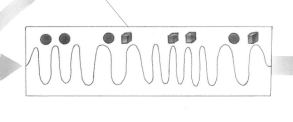

▲ *A computer connected to a modem (modulator-demodulator) can transmit signals through a telephone cable to another computer. The modem changes the signal from digital to analog.*

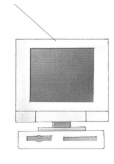

THE INTERNET

The Internet uses ordinary telephone lines to connect computers around the world in a giant network. People can exchange messages by electronic mail (e-mail), start a discussion group that anyone can join, post a notice on a global noticeboard, or find information on any topic.

▲ *New computerized route finders are being used to help drivers find the shortest route or the one with the least traffic.*

▶ *Cyber cafés are becoming increasingly popular. They enable people who don't have their own computers to "surf" the Internet to find information or send electronic mail.*

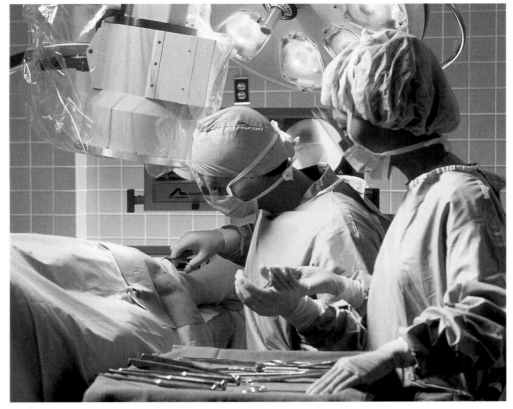

SURGERY
(*see* pages 80-81)

THE LIVING CELL
(*see* pages 70-71)

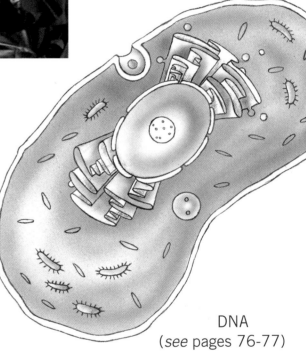

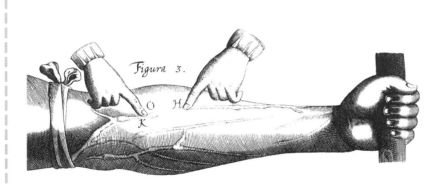

HISTORY OF
MEDICINE
(*see* pages 68-69)

DNA
(*see* pages 76-77)

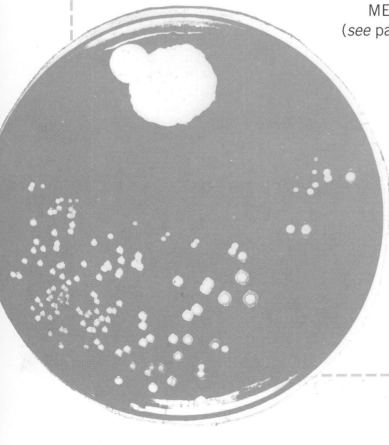

FIGHTING DISEASE
(*see* pages 78-79)

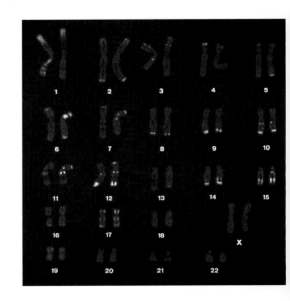

LEARNING ABOUT LIFE

Until about 300 years ago, little was known about how the body works, what causes disease, or how children inherit different traits from their mother and father.

In the last few decades, the knowledge of biology and medicine has grown beyond all recognition. Doctors understand more than ever before about viruses and other germs, curing disease, surgical processes and techniques, and how the billions of cells in the body operate and work together. They have learned that cells contain the blueprint of our bodies and how particular characteristics are reproduced.

Scientists are discovering and learning new things about the human body and how it functions all the time. They are even beginning to understand something about the fantastically complicated organ that controls memory and consciousness, emotion, and thought – the brain.

This section looks at the way our understanding of living organisms, including ourselves, has grown – sometimes in great leaps, but mostly in tiny steps, like evolution itself. Biological science is an area where progress is made all the time, but there is still a huge amount to be discovered and understood.

History of Medicine

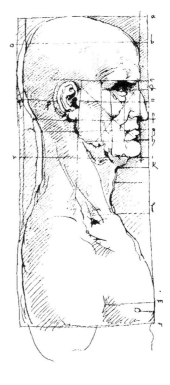

MEDICINE IS THE SCIENCE OF HEALING. For centuries people have tried to cure disease with varying degrees of success. The Chinese used herbs as drugs and inserted acupuncture needles into the body, practices that are still used in Chinese medicine today. Ancient Egyptians performed surgery using knives, forceps (pincers), and probes. The ancient Greeks studied anatomy, the brain, and nerves by cutting open dead animals and dissecting them, and in about 400 B.C. the Greek physician Hippocrates founded the first school of medicine.

Medical progress

For more than a thousand years medicine made no real progress in Europe because the Christian Church disapproved of dissection. Only from the 15th century were doctors able to investigate the structures inside the body. In 1543, a Belgian doctor named Andreas Vesalius published a revolutionary book on human anatomy based on his dissection of human bodies. The invention of the microscope helped to make further advances possible. Cells were first viewed through a microscope in 1665 and bacteria in 1676. Much later, in 1928, Alexander Fleming discovered penicillin, an antibiotic substance that kills most bacteria and can be used to fight infection.

▲ *Leonardo da Vinci was a painter, sculptor, architect, and engineer whose ideas were, in many cases, hundreds of years before their time. He drew anatomical pictures of dissected human corpses, and in so doing made discoveries about the structure of the body. This sketch shows the proportions of the head.*

◀ *Galen, a Greek who settled in Rome in about A.D. 170, developed widely accepted but mistaken theories about the functions of the body, such as the idea that spirits flowed through the arteries, veins, and nerves.*

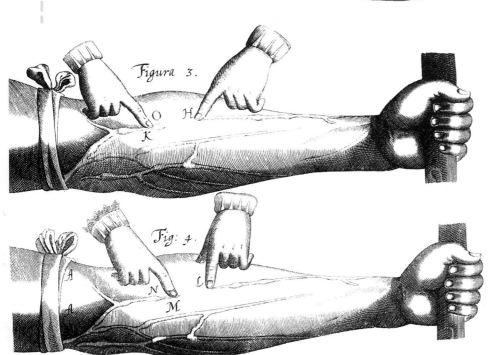

Figura 3.

Fig: 4.

◀ *William Harvey was an English doctor who studied the heart, veins, and arteries of living animals. In 1628 he showed how the heart pumps blood around the body. This drawing shows Harvey's demonstration of the existence of one-way valves in the main veins that stop blood from flowing the wrong way.*

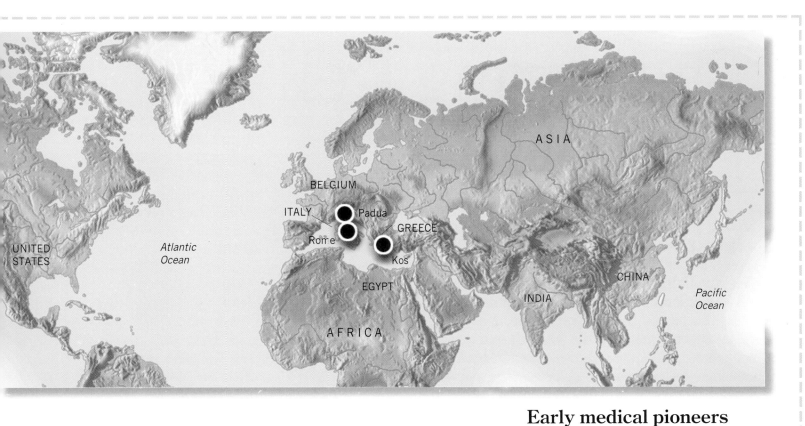

Early medical pioneers

Hippocrates worked at one of the earliest medical schools on the Greek island of Kos. Galen was also Greek, but became surgeon to the Roman gladiators and moved to Rome. Vesalius was a Belgian, who worked at the medical school in Padua, Italy.

MODERN MEDICINE

The use of drugs to fight disease has improved dramatically in the 20th century, as have other treatments such as radiotherapy – radiation used to destroy cancer tumors. There have been great improvements in diagnosing diseases too. X-rays, discovered in 1895, transformed medicine: for the first time, doctors could "see" inside the body. Now modern scanning methods can reveal much more detail inside the body, and can even show what is happening in the brain.

▲ *Florence Nightingale, the founder of modern nursing, tended the sick during the Crimean War in 1855. She revolutionized standards of cleanliness and trained nurses in proper patient care. The soldiers called her "the lady with the lamp" because she used to carry a lighted lamp with her as she walked around the wards at night.*

▶ *Doctors can use computer-generated images, such as this one showing a skull, to practice complicated surgical techniques.*

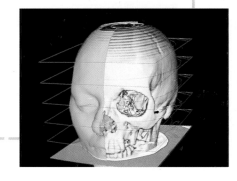

The Living Cell

THE INVENTION OF THE MICROSCOPE IN THE 1600S meant scientists could observe for the first time things that were too small to see with the naked eye. In 1665, English scientist Robert Hooke looked through a microscope and discovered that cork was made of many tiny compartments, which he called cells. A few years later Anton van Leeuwenhoek was able to watch blood flow through tiny blood vessels in a tadpole's tail, and found microscopic animals in stagnant water. In 1676 he saw bacteria through a microscope.

Biologists began to realize that all living organisms are made of cells. In 1838 a German doctor, Matthias Schleiden, recognized that cells are the basic parts of all plants. Another German doctor, Theodor Schwann, compared the structure and growth of animals and plants. He suggested that all animal tissues are made of cells, and that life begins with a single cell – the egg.

Discovery of chromosomes

In 1879, Walther Flemming used red dye to stain the nucleus of a cell, and saw how cells reproduce. He noticed tiny granules inside the nucleus. He called this grainy material chromatin (Greek for "color"). When the cell was about to divide, the chromatin lined up in threads, later called chromosomes (see page 75), and the nucleus dissolved. The chromosomes were pulled to the edges of the cell, half to each end. Then the cell pinched itself around its middle and split into two parts, and a new nucleus formed in each. Later, chromosomes were found to carry genetic code – information for the structure and growth of a body.

Pioneers in the discovery of cells

Two pioneers of work on cells were Anton van Leeuwenhoek, who worked in Delft in Holland in the 17th century, and Theodor Schwann, who worked on animal cells in Jena in Germany in the 19th century.

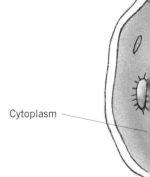

Cytoplasm

◀ *Anton van Leeuwenhoek, a Dutch merchant, used a microscope that could magnify objects 200 times.*

◀ *Red blood cells seen through a microscope. These doughnut-shaped cells carry life-giving oxygen from the lungs and release it into the body's tissues.*

ELECTRON MICROSCOPES

Instead of rays of light, electron microscopes send streams of electrons (see pages 26-27) through an object so that an image is produced on a video screen. Electrons can illuminate much smaller things than light can: some electron microscopes can magnify objects by more than a million times. The invention of the electron microscope enabled even the smallest details of the internal and external structure of cells to be thoroughly examined. This contributed greatly to the understanding of cell division and genetics (see page 74).

THE CELL

At its simplest, a cell consists of a sac with a thin outer plasma membrane containing the smaller, denser nucleus suspended in a jelly-like substance called cytoplasm. An average cell, such as a liver cell, is just 0.001 inches (0.03 mm) wide.

▼ *At the heart of an animal cell is the nucleus, which controls everything that happens inside the cell. Around the nucleus is the cytoplasm, which contains tiny structures, called organelles. Each kind of organelle carries out a different set of tasks. Mitochondria, for example, produce energy.*

▼ *Plant cells differ from animal cells in two important ways: they contain chloroplasts, which give them their green color, and they have a stiff cell wall.*

The endoplasmic reticulum is a system of double membranes on which chemical reactions take place.

Mitochondria   Chloroplast   Nucleus

Cytoplasm

Cell membrane   Vacuoles are storage areas in the cell.   Cell wall

▶ *The cells of bacteria and other micro-organisms do not have nuclei or mitochondria.*

Molecule of DNA

Cytoplasm

Cell membrane

Cell wall

Flagella enable the cell to move

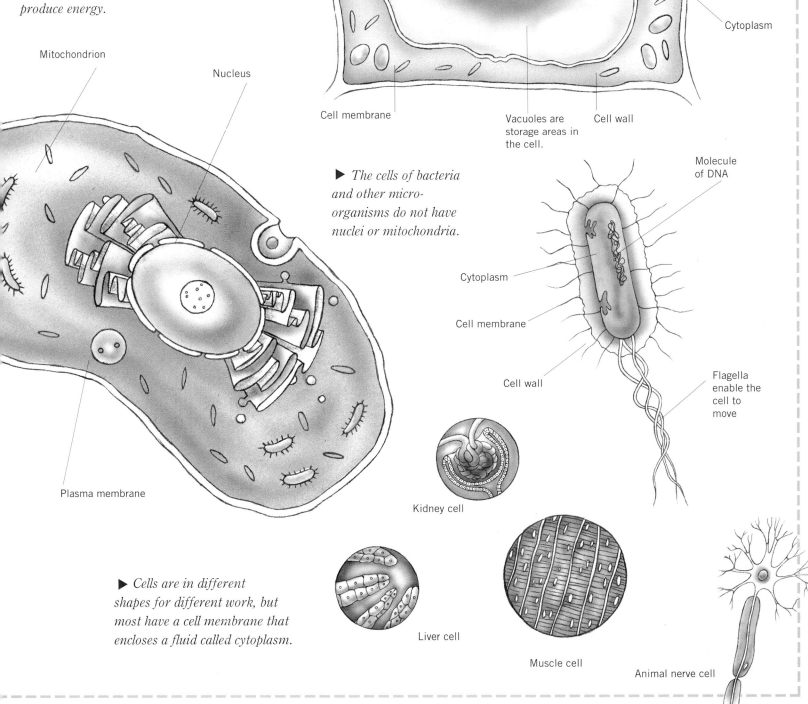

Mitochondrion   Nucleus

Plasma membrane

Kidney cell

▶ *Cells are in different shapes for different work, but most have a cell membrane that encloses a fluid called cytoplasm.*

Liver cell

Muscle cell

Animal nerve cell

Evolution

PROF. DARWIN.
This is the ape of form.
Love's Labor Lost, act 5, scene 2.
Some four or five descents since.
All's Well that Ends Well, act 3, sc. 7.

UNTIL THE 19TH CENTURY most people believed that the Earth was only a few thousand years old and that all living things had been specially created. However, some people began to doubt this, and eventually the idea of evolution came about. Evolution is the idea that animals and plants are descended from earlier species and have slowly changed over millions of years.

People once believed that new animals and plants came into being as a result of catastrophes on Earth. In the 18th century, Charles Lyell became convinced that it was natural forces, such as weather and tides, not catastrophes, that gradually shaped the Earth over an extremely long time and that animals and plants slowly adapted, too.

Darwin and Malthus

Lyell's ideas influenced a young naturalist named Charles Darwin, who was also influenced by the ideas of Thomas Malthus, who had written a book about populations in which he pointed out that if conditions were perfect, the animal population would grow until there was no more room on the planet. This does not happen only because there are limits, such as food shortage and illness.

In 1859, Darwin published his famous book, *On the Origin of Species*. In it he put forward his theories of evolution based on his observations as a naturalist aboard the HMS *Beagle*, on its round-the-world voyage of 1838.

▲ *This cartoon was typical of the negative reaction to Darwin's theory of evolution. Many people misinterpreted what Darwin said, and thought that he was claiming that humans were the direct descendants of monkeys.*

◀ *Charles Darwin proposed the idea of natural selection: that only the fittest survive.*

THE GALAPAGOS FINCHES

In the Galápagos Islands, Charles Darwin was struck by the different types of finches he saw. There were at least fourteen different species of varying sizes. Each had a different color and shape of beak. Some ate seeds or cactus plants, while others ate insects. These varieties were not found anywhere else, although there was one close relative on the mainland. Darwin realized that the finches must originally have come from the mainland. As they grew in number, their food supplies diminished. Only the most efficient – the fittest – survived. These survivors were stronger or ate other types of food. By passing this trait on to their offspring, they would ensure the survival of the species. Darwin called this idea "natural selection."

Long thin beak for getting insects out of tree bark

Large strong beak for breaking open shellfish

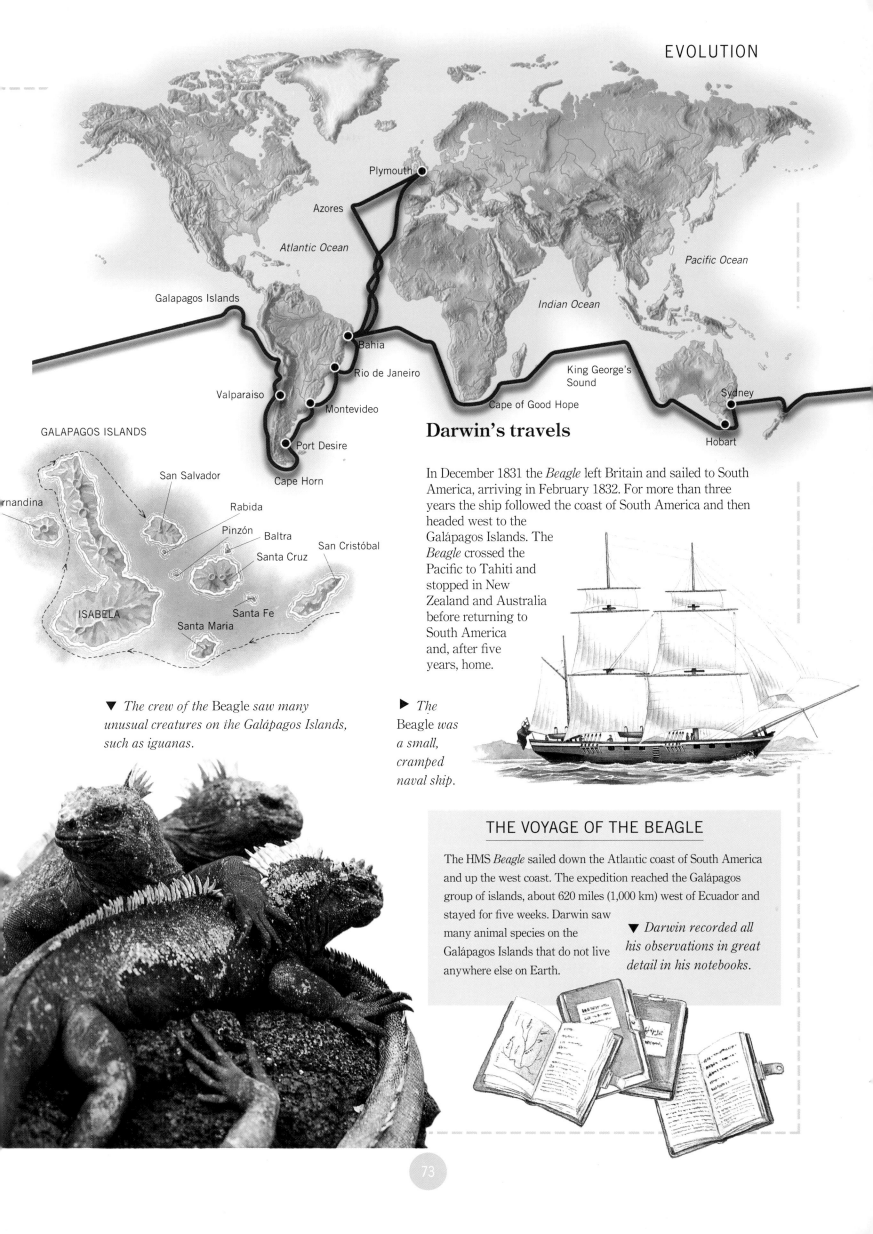

Plymouth

Azores

Atlantic Ocean

Pacific Ocean

Galapagos Islands

Indian Ocean

Bahia

Rio de Janeiro

King George's
Sound

Sydney

Valparaiso

Montevideo

Cape of Good Hope

Hobart

GALAPAGOS ISLANDS

Port Desire

Cape Horn

nandina

San Salvador

Rabida

Pinzón

Baltra

San Cristóbal

Santa Cruz

ISABELA

Santa Fe

Santa Maria

Darwin's travels

In December 1831 the *Beagle* left Britain and sailed to South America, arriving in February 1832. For more than three years the ship followed the coast of South America and then headed west to the Galápagos Islands. The *Beagle* crossed the Pacific to Tahiti and stopped in New Zealand and Australia before returning to South America and, after five years, home.

▼ *The crew of the* Beagle *saw many unusual creatures on the Galápagos Islands, such as iguanas.*

▶ *The* Beagle *was a small, cramped naval ship.*

THE VOYAGE OF THE BEAGLE

The HMS *Beagle* sailed down the Atlantic coast of South America and up the west coast. The expedition reached the Galápagos group of islands, about 620 miles (1,000 km) west of Ecuador and stayed for five weeks. Darwin saw many animal species on the Galápagos Islands that do not live anywhere else on Earth.

▼ *Darwin recorded all his observations in great detail in his notebooks.*

Genetics

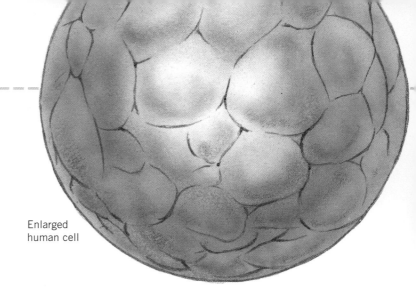

Enlarged human cell

FOR CENTURIES, FARMERS HAVE BRED selected animals and plants to try to improve them, and to create strains with particular characteristics. However it wasn't until 1865, when an Austrian monk called Gregor Mendel began to experiment with pea plants in his monastery garden, that the rules of genetics – the way in which all living things inherit characteristics from their parents – were worked out. Mendel discovered that each characteristic of a living thing is controlled by one factor – a gene. Genes are arranged in pairs. Only one of each pair is passed on from each parent to its offspring. Mendel also realized that usually one gene of each pair is dominant, meaning it hides the effect of the other gene.

Human genes

Humans have about 100,000 genes. Most human characteristics are not a simple result of one gene (though some, such as eye color are); they are a result of several genes acting together. Genetics explains why each individual in every generation of every species is slightly different. But genes are not the only factor that determine the way we are. Our personalities are almost certainly a combination of inherited genes and the environment in which we grow up.

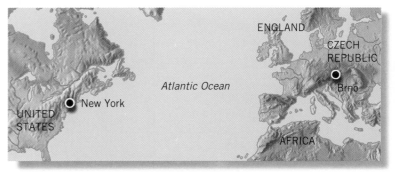

Genetic discoveries

Fifty years after Mendel's experiments at Brno (now in the Czech Republic), American biologist William Morgan continued research into genetics in New York. His experiments with fruit flies revealed that inherited characteristics are sometimes linked to the sex of the parent.

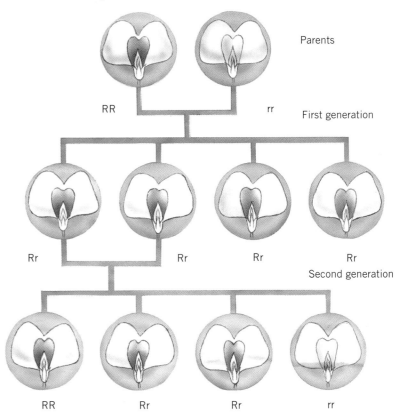

Parents

RR   rr   First generation

Rr   Rr   Rr   Rr
Second generation

RR   Rr   Rr   rr

▲ *Dominant genes are labeled R. Recessive genes (labeled r) only show if there are two plants with them, which is why these parents (top) produce all red offspring. The second generation may produce at least one flower with white leaves – because more than two of their parents had recessive white genes.*

MENDEL'S PEA PLANTS

In one experiment, Mendel worked with sweet pea plants. He crossed plants whose flowers were red with plants that produced white flowers.

In the next generation, the flowers were not a mixture of colors – they were all red. When these offspring produced flowers, most flowers were red, but almost one-fourth of the flowers were white. The red gene is dominant, so if a plant had one red gene and one white, its flowers would be red. Only the plants with two white genes had white flowers.

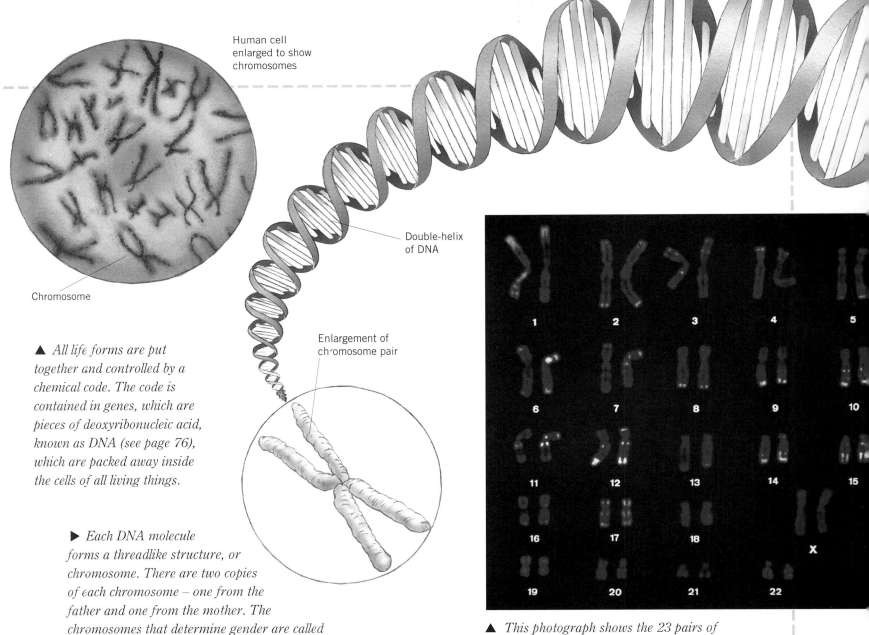

Human cell enlarged to show chromosomes

Chromosome

Double-helix of DNA

Enlargement of chromosome pair

▲ *All life forms are put together and controlled by a chemical code. The code is contained in genes, which are pieces of deoxyribonucleic acid, known as DNA (see page 76), which are packed away inside the cells of all living things.*

▶ *Each DNA molecule forms a threadlike structure, or chromosome. There are two copies of each chromosome – one from the father and one from the mother. The chromosomes that determine gender are called sex chromosomes – females have two X sex chromosomes and males have one X and one Y.*

1 2 3 4 5

6 7 8 9 10

11 12 13 14 15

16 17 18 X

19 20 21 22

▲ *This photograph shows the 23 pairs of human chromosomes contained in a single human cell. The sex chromosomes – here both labeled X (female) – are on the lower right.*

HEMOPHILIA

Hemophilia is a disorder that prevents the blood from clotting. It is normally caused by a defective gene on the male X chromosome – which means that men get the disease and women (who have a spare X chromosome with no defect) are the carriers. Like color blindness, it is a rescessive gene – which means that it does not appear in every generation. In the 19th and 20th centuries, hemophilia was passed from mothers to sons through many European royal families.

◀ *Hemophilia was passed to Alexis (far right), Czar Nicholas II of Russia's son, by his mother, Empress Alexandra.*

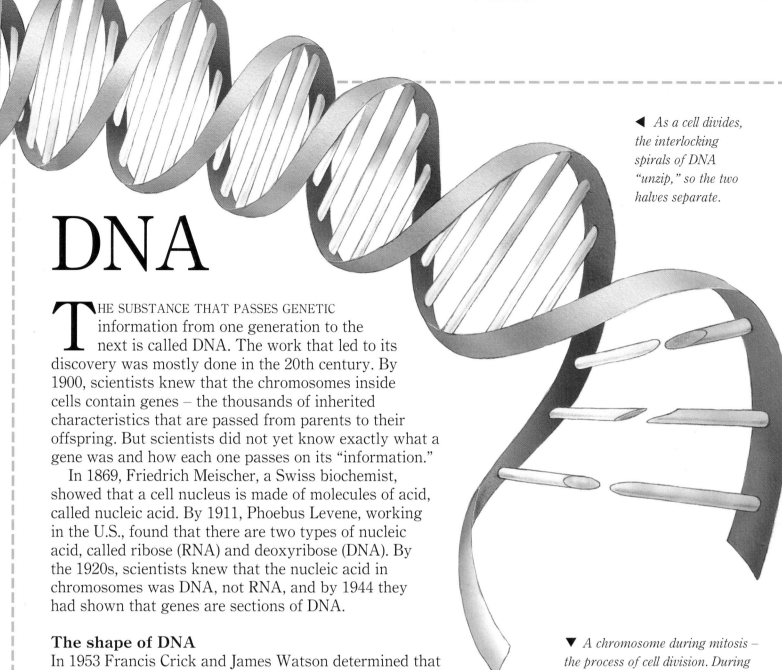

DNA

T HE SUBSTANCE THAT PASSES GENETIC information from one generation to the next is called DNA. The work that led to its discovery was mostly done in the 20th century. By 1900, scientists knew that the chromosomes inside cells contain genes – the thousands of inherited characteristics that are passed from parents to their offspring. But scientists did not yet know exactly what a gene was and how each one passes on its "information."

In 1869, Friedrich Meischer, a Swiss biochemist, showed that a cell nucleus is made of molecules of acid, called nucleic acid. By 1911, Phoebus Levene, working in the U.S., found that there are two types of nucleic acid, called ribose (RNA) and deoxyribose (DNA). By the 1920s, scientists knew that the nucleic acid in chromosomes was DNA, not RNA, and by 1944 they had shown that genes are sections of DNA.

◄ As a cell divides, the interlocking spirals of DNA "unzip," so the two halves separate.

The shape of DNA

In 1953 Francis Crick and James Watson determined that the shape of DNA is a double helix – a shape rather like a spiral staircase made up of two interlocking ropes. The shape explained how DNA could copy itself as cells divided in order to pass on information. The DNA "unzips" itself – as if the "rungs" on the ladder are sawn in half – and the halves separate. From chemicals floating around in the cell, each half makes itself a partner to form a complete double helix again, making two perfect copies of the original. In the 1970s, scientists found out how to use special proteins called enzymes as scissors, to "snip" genes, and other enzymes to join lengths of genes back together. This gave them the ability to change or even create genes, and led to a new technology: genetic engineering.

▼ A chromosome during mitosis – the process of cell division. During mitosis a duplicate set of the parent cell's genes is produced, so that both offspring have identical gene pairs.

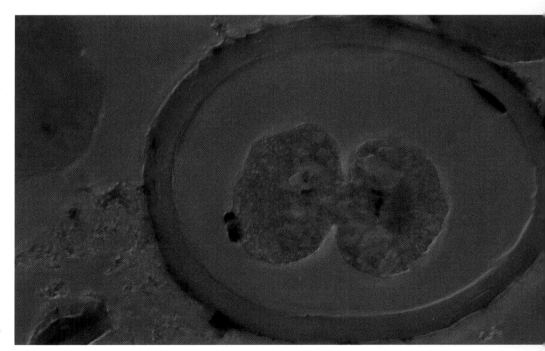

"IMPROVING" ON NATURE

With the discovery of DNA came the ability, in the 1970s, to alter the genes of an organism in order to change its characteristics. Genetic engineering is now being used to create better strains of crop plants. This can be done, for instance, by transferring a gene that protects one plant against insect attack into another plant.

▲ *A genetically altered cotton plant.*

▲ *The tomatoes on the right have been genetically altered to keep them fresh for longer.*

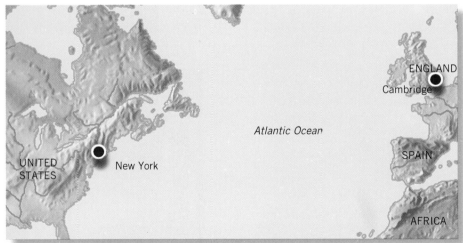

◄ *This photograph shows American James Watson (far right), and British scientist Francis Crick (third from left) at the Nobel Prize award ceremony in 1962.*

USES OF DNA

In the same way that each person has unique fingerprints, so each of us has a different pattern of DNA. Since 1984, forensic scientists have used a test known as DNA profiling. Suspect criminals can be identified by the DNA in material such as blood, saliva, or hair.

Begun in the 1980s, the Human Genome Project aims to build a computer map of all the genes in the body and eventually to work out what each one does. Geneticists hope to use the information to cure genetic diseases that are passed on from one generation to the next, such as hemophilia (*see* page 75).

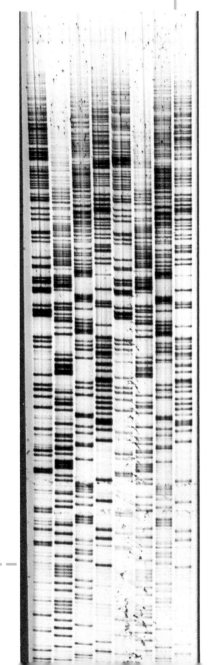

▶ *This picture shows "sequencing gels," the basic technology used to map the genetic sequences of human genes.*

The discovery of DNA

In 1944, three American scientists Oswald Avery, Colin Macleod, and Maclyn McCarty working in New York, were the first to discover that genes are made of DNA. In the 1950s, James Watson and Francis Crick did their pioneering investigation of the structure of DNA at Cambridge, England.

Fighting Disease

SINCE THE FIRST VACCINE WAS DISCOVERED in the 18th century, millions of lives have been saved by these simple cures. Vaccination works by preparing someone's body to fight a particular disease by giving them a weakened, harmless dose of that disease before they are infected by the real thing.

An English doctor, Edward Jenner, discovered the first vaccine, for smallpox, in 1796. Smallpox was then a common disease, which caused blindness and disfigurement. Yet experience showed that once it had struck, that person never caught it again. Jenner decided to deliberately infect a boy with the related but harmless disease cowpox. When the boy was well again, Jenner infected him with smallpox. The smallpox did not take effect, because the milder illness had made the boy immune.

Vaccines have now wiped out smallpox entirely. There are also vaccines against many other diseases, such as polio, measles, mumps, and rabies.

Jenner did not realize it, but he was fighting a virus. Viruses are single strands of DNA or RNA (*see* pages 76-77) enclosed by a layer of protein. Viruses cannot live on their own, but depend on the cells they invade. They are too small to be seen in an ordinary microscope – about 1/1000th the size of a bacterium. Vaccination is the only defence against viruses.

Bacteria and antibiotics

Bacteria are microscopic single-celled organisms. They were first seen through microscopes in the late 17th century. Bacteria were later realized to cause diseases. The bacteria that cause tuberculosis, cholera, and diphtheria were all discovered in the 1880s, but a cure was not found until 1928. The Scottish doctor Alexander Fleming discovered that penicillin was a powerful weapon against bacteria.

▲ *This picture, from a French magazine of 1912, shows the Turkish army defeated not by the enemy, but by a water-borne disease called cholera.*

LOUIS PASTEUR

Louis Pasteur was the first person to connect bacteria with infection. In 1865 he helped rescue the French silk industry, which was being ruined by a silkworm disease. He found bacteria infecting both the worms and the leaves they ate. When the infected worms and leaves were destroyed, the disease died out. Once Pasteur proved that diseases were spread by bacteria, hygiene was taken more seriously.

Pasteur also proved that food rots because of bacteria in the air. He discovered a way of heating milk that kills the dangerous bacteria that make it go bad. This process is named for him – pasteurization. He discovered, too, that weakened bacteria could be used as vaccines, just like weakened viruses. He made new anti-virus vaccines as well. In 1885 he injected a young boy who had been bitten by a rabid dog with weakened rabies bacteria. The vaccination succeeded, and the boy survived.

▲ *Louis Pasteur was a brilliant chemist and microbiologist.*

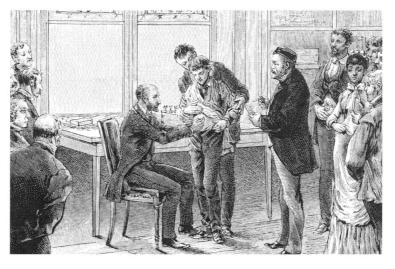

◀ *Louis Pasteur watches a boy being vaccinated against rabies.*

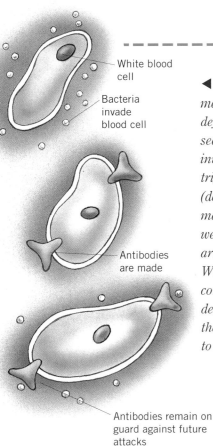

White blood cell

Bacteria invade blood cell

Antibodies are made

Antibodies remain on guard against future attacks

◀ *The body's defense mechanism consists of defender cells that seek out bacteria invaders. Vaccines trigger antibodies (destroyer cells) to be made even though the weakened invaders are no real threat. When the real thing comes along, the destroyer cells are there already, waiting to attack.*

ENGLAND
Berkeley
London
Paris
FRANCE

Fighting disease

Jenner worked at Berkeley, England, in the 18th century, while Pasteur studied microbes and diseases in Paris in the 19th century. In the 20th century Fleming discovered penicillin in London.

▲ *Edward Jenner, an English country doctor, pioneered vaccination.*

▶ *The body's natural defenses help fight infection. If a splinter pierces the skin (right), a blood clot heals the wound and blood cells called macrophages remove wound debris such as dried blood (far right).*

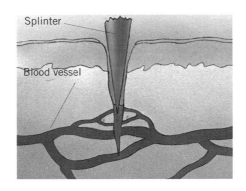

Splinter

Blood vessel

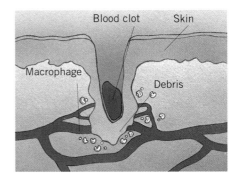

Blood clot   Skin

Macrophage

Debris

FLEMING AND PENICILLIN

Alexander Fleming (1881-1955) spent many years looking for substances that would fight bacteria. In 1921 he discovered that tears and saliva both contain a protein that kills some germs. In 1928 he discovered the first antibiotic drug, penicillin, in mold. This powerful chemical inhibited the growth of bacteria. Fleming discovered penicillin, but it was two other scientists, Howard Florey, an Australian doctor, and Ernst Chain, a German chemist, who first used it to fight infection. Penicillin was effectively put to use during World War II to treat soldiers' wounds.

By 1945 enough penicillin was being made to treat 250,000 patients.

Soon other antibiotics were discovered in molds in soil. For the last 50 years these drugs have been relied upon to cure infectious diseases.

◀ *Alexander Fleming working in a hospital laboratory.*

▼ *Laboratory work on new antibiotics in California.*

◀ *The original plate on which Fleming first observed penicillin.*

Surgery

THOUSANDS OF YEARS AGO, SURGEONS WERE PERFORMING operations in India and Ancient Egypt. They used surgical instruments similar to those used today. For centuries, though, any operation, no matter how vital, was as likely to kill the patient through pain and shock as it was to cure.

In 1799, Sir Humphry Davy, an English scientist, made a gas called nitrous oxide, or "laughing gas." It was first used in 1844 as an anesthetic (meaning "no feeling") by Horace Wells, an American dentist. In 1846 another gas, ether, was used in surgery. It lasted longer than nitrous oxide and could put a patient to sleep. Also that year a Scottish surgeon, James Simpson, used chloroform gas administered through a mask over the patient's face. It worked better than ether, with fewer side effects. Modern anesthetics are very sophisticated. Some act locally, numbing parts of the body without putting the patient to sleep. Drugs can even stop muscles trembling during surgery.

Advances in hygiene were also being made. In 1865, Joseph Lister of London began using chemicals, such as carbolic acid spray, to kill germs in the air and in the patient's wounds. By the end of the 19th century, surgeons were wearing clean white gowns, thin rubber gloves, and gauze masks, and were sterilizing their equipment in order to prevent germs infecting the patient.

Modern surgery

Today, machines constantly monitor the activity of the heart, lungs, and brain during surgery to make sure everything goes smoothly. Many operations that used to mean opening up the body can now be performed using ultrasound beams or lasers. Soon miniature robots will help brain surgeons to guide their instruments more carefully than hands ever could.

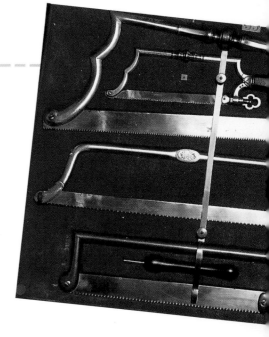

▲ *These surgical instruments were used in the early 18th century. At this time, surgeons were saw doctors: little more than a cross between a barber and a butcher! The instruments shown include a saw with a screw for tightening the blade and a small saw for amputating fingers and toes.*

▼ *Microsurgery can be performed using microscopes and fine tools to mend nerves or repair holes in a baby's heart – an operation that has even been performed while the baby was still in its mother's womb.*

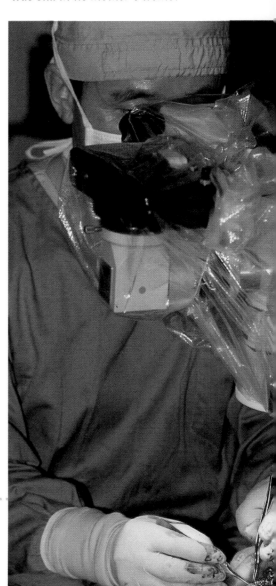

▼ *The photograph below shows an operation in progress during the 1870s.*

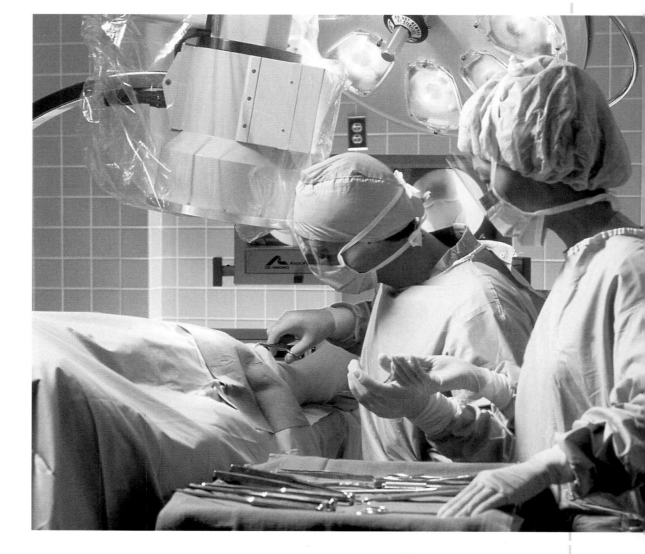

▶ *In a modern operating theater a number of people, including the surgeon, an anesthetist, nurses, and theater technicians work together as a team.*

▼ *The endoscope is an optical device that is inserted through a small hole in the skin in order to see inside the body. Modern endoscopes incorporate bundles of optical fibers and lasers for peering through "keyhole" incisions in the body.*

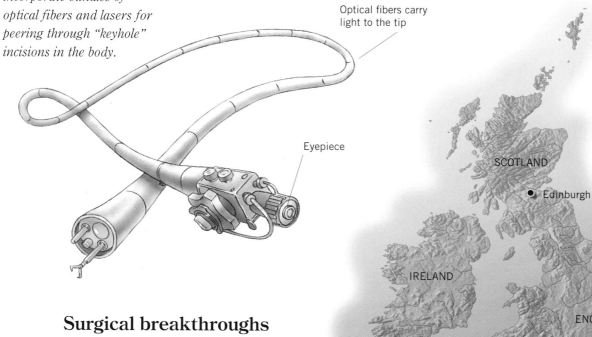

Optical fibers carry light to the tip

Eyepiece

SCOTLAND
• Edinburgh

IRELAND

ENGLAND

• Bristol

Penzance •

Surgical breakthroughs

Sir Humphry Davy originally came from Penzance in Cornwall, but it was while working in a laboratory in Bristol that he discovered that nitrous oxide could be used as an anesthetic. In 1847 in Edinburgh, Scottish surgeon James Simpson discovered that chloroform could also be used as an anesthetic.

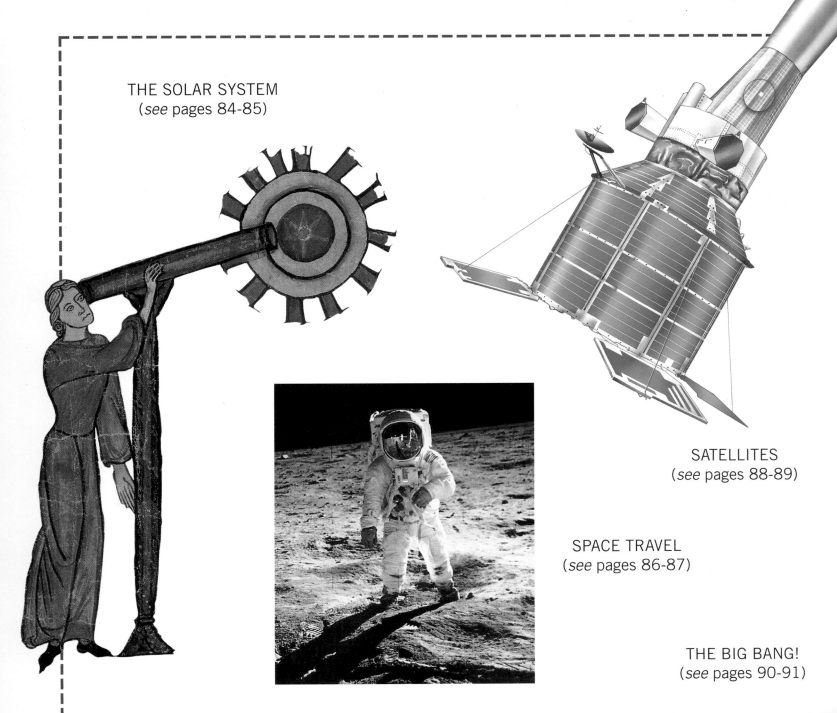

THE SOLAR SYSTEM
(*see* pages 84-85)

SATELLITES
(*see* pages 88-89)

SPACE TRAVEL
(*see* pages 86-87)

THE BIG BANG!
(*see* pages 90-91)

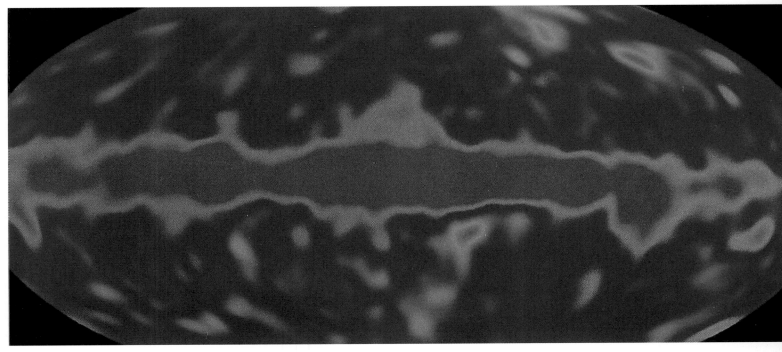

ASTRONOMY AND COSMOLOGY

People in early civilizations had ideas about the Sun and the Moon, but they were held back by many confusing and widely held myths and legends about what the moving lights and patterns in the sky meant.

With the invention of the astronomical telescope in 1609, the stars and planets became easier to study. Scientific observations indicated that the the Earth was not the center of the Universe, as was previously thought. Like the other planets, it revolved around the Sun.

The 20th century saw a dramatic increase in astronomical research. Astronomy (the study of stars) and cosmology (the study of the Universe) keep revealing new questions, as well as answers.

In this final section, you can read about how so much was discovered about the Universe just by looking and thinking hard about ways to explain what was seen. This section also tells the story of space travel, with spacecraft now carrying cameras and other instruments to the outer reaches of the solar system. Satellites have also led to a new understanding of our world and our environment.

The Solar System

FROM EARLIEST TIMES, PEOPLE HAVE contemplated the heavens. The ancient civilizations of Egypt, Babylon, India, and China each had its own system of astronomy. They made observations of stars, comets, eclipses, and the phases of the Moon, and used them to make calendars and to predict the seasons.

The most puzzling elements in the sky were the "wandering stars" – the planets, the Sun, and the Moon. Most Greek philosophers thought that the Earth was at the center of the Universe, and that the planets moved in perfect circles.

In 1543 a Polish astronomer, Nicolaus Copernicus, published a book that broke 1,500 years of tradition. It stated that the planets, including Earth, revolved around the Sun; only the Moon circled the Earth.

In 1609, an Italian scientist named Galileo Galilei used the telescope, which had recently been invented, to make astronomical observations that astonished the scientific world. He saw the surface of the Moon, the crescent phases of Venus, rings around Saturn, and moons revolving around Jupiter. All he saw indicated that Copernicus was right: the Earth was not the center of the Universe. This provoked a strong reaction from the Church because Galileo's findings contradicted the Bible, and he was declared a heretic.

At the same time, Johannes Kepler in Germany worked out that the planets really moved not in circles but in ellipses – elongated circles. Later, Sir Isaac Newton's theory of gravity (*see* pages 24-25) helped explain how the planets are held in their orbits.

DISCOVERING THE PLANETS

Until the 18th century, astronomers thought that Saturn was the most distant planet. But in 1781 the German astronomer William Herschel observed a faint star moving against the background stars. It turned out to be the planet Uranus. He also discovered a mass of rock fragments, called asteroids, that orbit the Sun between Mars and Jupiter. An eighth planet, Neptune, was discovered in 1846, and a ninth, Pluto, in 1930.

◀ *William Herschel was the first man to record the approximate shape of our galaxy, the Milky Way.*

▲ *Telescopes were invented early in the 17th century by a Dutch lens maker named Hans Lippershey. But the Italian Galileo was the first person to look at the night sky with one.*

PTOLEMY

Ptolemy was the leading Greek astronomer of the 2nd century A.D. He believed that the Earth was fixed at the center of the Universe, and the stars revolved around it. If the Earth revolved, he argued, birds would fall out of the trees. This view became the official teaching of the Christian Church, and was accepted by Arabian and European scholars until the end of the medieval period, in the 16th century.

▲ *This depiction of the Ptolemaic system of the Universe shows the positions of the Sun, Moon, and planets.*

▲ *This imaginative reconstruction shows the Greek astronomer Ptolemy in his observatory in Alexandria, Egypt, where he lived.*

Astronomical breakthroughs

An early observatory was built at the Mayan city of Chichén Itzá in Mexico. Ptolemy lived in Alexandria, Egypt, about 124 miles (200 km) north of the Giza Pyramids. Galileo first used his telescope in Venice, Italy, and he was sent to Rome to be tried for heresy. Kepler, in Prague, the capital of the Czech Republic, observed elliptical orbits.

▶ *The Ancient Egyptians built their pyramids and temples so that the sides were aligned north-south and east-west. To do this, they used their detailed knowledge of the positions of the stars and planets.*

◀ *Astronomers observe the sky from a tower in Constantinople (modern Istanbul), in this 16th-century painting. Arab culture flourished from the 7th century. Astronomy was one of the subjects studied at Muslim universities.*

85

Space Travel

THE FATHER OF SPACEFLIGHT WAS A RUSSIAN, Konstantin Tsiolkovsky. He had the original idea for multistage rocket motors. In order to overcome the force of gravity, rockets have to reach a speed of 25,000 mph (40,000 km/h), which is called the escape velocity. Rockets need several motors to reach this velocity. At each stage, a motor burns all its fuel and then drops off, leaving the rocket lighter, but with the remaining fuel tanks full.

In 1926, Robert Goddard in the United States made the first successful liquid-fueled rockets. Soon afterward, the Germans, under a brilliant young engineer named Werner von Braun, were hard at work on rockets. Rocket weapons were used against London in the last months of World War II. After the war, von Braun and his colleagues went to the United States, and the race to space began.

The Russians won the race when they launched *Sputnik 1* in 1957 (*see* pages 88-89), but the Americans were the first to put men on the Moon, on July 20, 1969, with *Apollo 11*. Since then, European countries, as well as India, Canada, China, and Japan, have developed their own space programs.

In 1981, the first space shuttle, *Columbia*, was launched. Space shuttles are designed to return to space again and again. They carry crews of up to seven men or women, and are mainly used for launching satellites and for zero gravity research.

MANNED SPACEFLIGHT

The Russian Yuri Gagarin was the first man to orbit the Earth and experience the weightlessness of zero gravity. His historic flight took place on April 12, 1961, in the 5-ton spacecraft *Vostok 1*. He attained a height of 188 miles (300 km) during his 1-hour-and-29-minute orbit and landed safely.

◀ Apollo 11 *cleared its mobile launcher to begin its journey to the Moon on July 16, 1969.*

▲ *The Russian cosmonaut Yuri Gagarin is dressed in his training suit on the left. Modern space suits have become much more elaborate.*

▼ *The* Apollo *spacecraft was launched by an airborne Saturn V rocket* ❶*, and it entered Earth's orbit* ❷ *. The spacecraft then split up again* ❸ *, giving an extra boost to the command and service modules (CSM) and lunar modules (LM) in order to boost them* ❹ *to the Moon. The LM landed* ❺ *, while the CSM stayed in orbit* ❻ *. On the homeward bound journey, the top half of the LM left the Moon* ❼ *and docked with the CSM* ❽ *. The command (crew) module separated* ❾ *, then parachuted down to land in the ocean* ❿ *.*

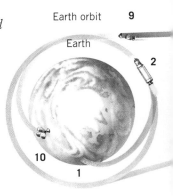

Earth orbit 9

Earth

◀ *The Chinese were the first to fire rockets. They discovered gunpowder in about A.D. 850. In the 13th century they used rockets – like modern fireworks – to frighten their enemies.*

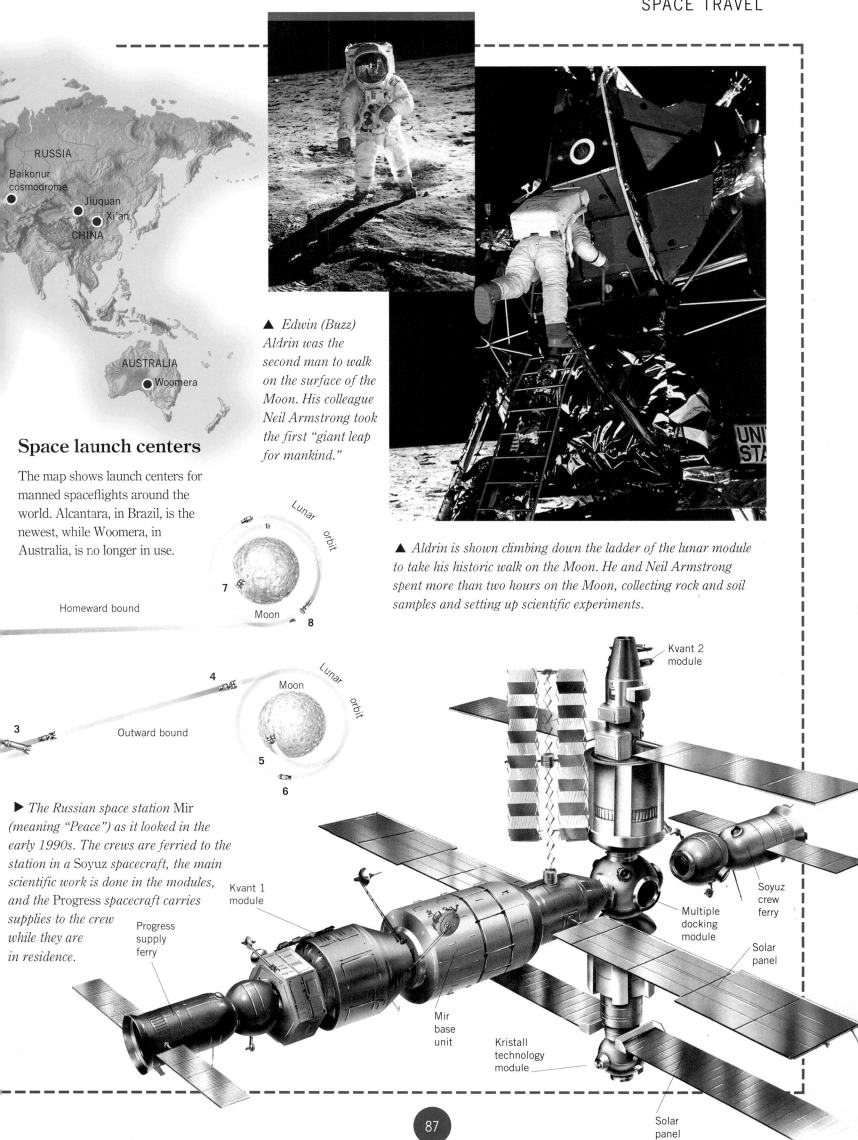

▲ *Edwin (Buzz) Aldrin was the second man to walk on the surface of the Moon. His colleague Neil Armstrong took the first "giant leap for mankind."*

Space launch centers

The map shows launch centers for manned spaceflights around the world. Alcantara, in Brazil, is the newest, while Woomera, in Australia, is no longer in use.

▲ *Aldrin is shown climbing down the ladder of the lunar module to take his historic walk on the Moon. He and Neil Armstrong spent more than two hours on the Moon, collecting rock and soil samples and setting up scientific experiments.*

▶ *The Russian space station* Mir *(meaning "Peace") as it looked in the early 1990s. The crews are ferried to the station in a* Soyuz *spacecraft, the main scientific work is done in the modules, and the* Progress *spacecraft carries supplies to the crew while they are in residence.*

Satellites

THE WORLD'S FIRST SATELLITE, *SPUTNIK 1*, WAS launched by the former Soviet Union on October 4, 1957. The American *Explorer 1* followed in January 1958. Soon satellites had begun to change the world.

During the Cold War, satellites were used by the United States and the former Soviet Union to spy on each other. Satellite "intelligence" was also used during the Gulf War and is vital to modern warfare.

Weather observation satellites beam pictures from their vantage point high above the Earth. The pictures show clouds, winds, and other weather systems, and are an invaluable tool for forecasters.

Environmental resource satellites map the Earth's surface. They monitor the climate by detecting changes in water flow, snow or ice cover, or the desert. They can spot sites likely to hold underground mineral or oil reserves, or detect how land is being used. At sea, satellites can pick out water currents and the movements of fish. They can map forests and forest clearance, and detect forest fires as soon as they break out. In short, much more is known about our planet, its atmosphere, oceans, and land than would have been possible without satellites.

Satellites have also revolutionized communications. They carry thousands of channels of telephone, fax, television, radio, and computer data, bringing the world closer together than ever before.

▼ *This American early warning satellite is fitted with an infrared telescope 13 feet (4 meters) long to detect missile launches from the former Soviet Union.*

UNITED STATES

Vandenberg

▼ *Satellites can detect what kind of crop is growing in a particular field and whether it is healthy or diseased by providing photographs like this.*

ARTHUR C. CLARKE

In 1945, long before the first spacecraft was launched, the science-fiction writer Arthur C. Clarke had an idea. Why not use artificial satellites to relay radio signals from continent to continent? The idea seemed impossible at the time, but 14 years later the first satellites were in orbit. He was even sent a message of appreciation when Neil Armstrong returned to Earth from his historic Moon landing in 1969.

ARTHUR C. CLARKE
BESTSELLING AUTHOR OF 2010: ODYSSEY TWO
THE SENTINEL
SUPERB SCIENCE FICTION – SUPERBLY ILLUSTRATED

▶ *Arthur C. Clarke is an engineer who is better known for his science-fiction novels. His short story* The Sentinel *was adapted for the movie* 2001 – A Space Odyssey.

SKYLAB

Skylab, the first manned space station, was launched on May 14, 1973. It was designed to accommodate three astronauts and carried an extensive array of scientific equipment. Three teams of astronauts carried out valuable experiments during their respective 28-, 59-, and 84-day expeditions. The space station reentered the Earth's atmosphere and burnt up over Australia in July 1979.

▶ *This photograph taken from onboard* Skylab *shows the space station cluster orbiting Earth.*

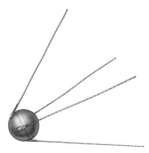

▲ Sputnik 1, *which carried little more than a radio transmitter, orbitted the Earth until early 1958.* Sputnik *in Russian means "traveling companion."*

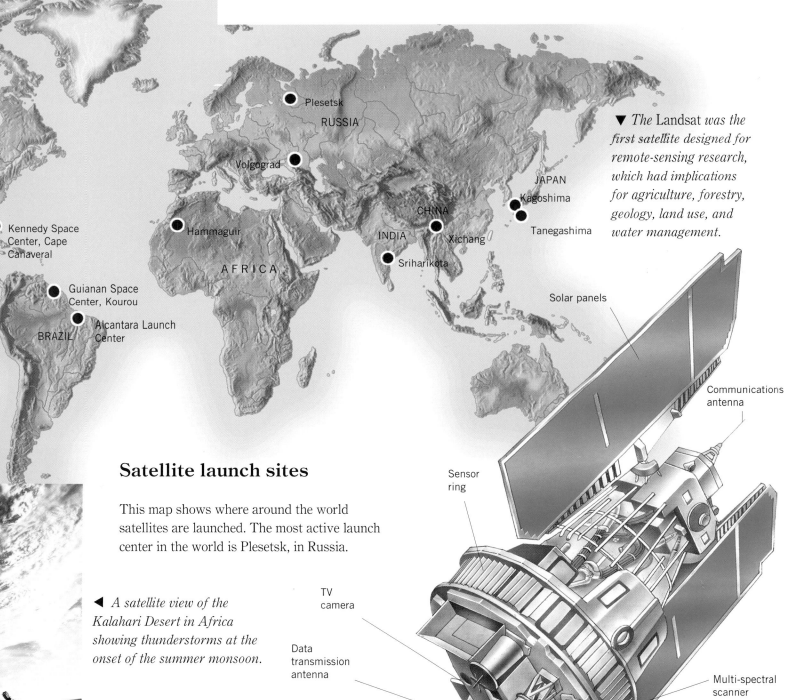

Plesetsk

RUSSIA

Volgograd

JAPAN

Kagoshima

CHINA

Kennedy Space Center, Cape Canaveral

Hammaguir

INDIA

Xichang

Tanegashima

AFRICA

Sriharikota

Guianan Space Center, Kourou

Alcantara Launch Center

BRAZIL

▼ *The* Landsat *was the first satellite designed for remote-sensing research, which had implications for agriculture, forestry, geology, land use, and water management.*

Solar panels

Communications antenna

Satellite launch sites

This map shows where around the world satellites are launched. The most active launch center in the world is Plesetsk, in Russia.

Sensor ring

◀ *A satellite view of the Kalahari Desert in Africa showing thunderstorms at the onset of the summer monsoon.*

TV camera

Data transmission antenna

Multi-spectral scanner

The Big Bang!

IN THE 1920S THE ASTRONOMER EDWIN HUBBLE noticed that all stars, except for the nearest few, are flying away from Earth at high speed. He observed that the further a star is from the Sun, the faster it is retreating. He had discovered that the whole Universe, including space itself, is expanding.

This led to the Big Bang theory, which was put forward by astronomers such as Russian-American George Gamow to explain the origin of the Universe. They said that all matter and energy was created in a vast explosion 15,000 million years ago, and has been moving apart ever since.

A second theory, the steady-state model, said that new galaxies are being created continually to keep the Universe at a constant density. The Universe did not have a beginning – it has always looked as it does now and always will.

Both theories seemed plausible. Then, in 1964, two American physicists, Arno Penzias and Robert Wilson, were using radio detection equipment when they found a persistent radio "noise." This was later determined to be the background radiation left over from the Big Bang. Further evidence for the Big Bang came from the Cosmic Background Explorer (COBE) satellite in 1992, which detected ripples in the background radiation.

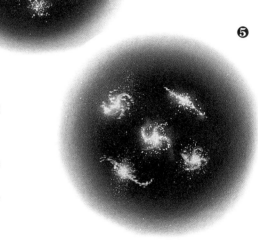

❷ ❸ ❹ ❶ ❺

THE END OF THE UNIVERSE

If the Universe had a beginning, will it have an end? Some astronomers think that the universe is "closed." According to this theory, the Universe will begin to shrink in on itself once it can expand no further, until it finally collapses in a "big crunch." Another possibility is that the Universe is "open." Everything will continue to move apart until the spaces between galaxies are huge and all the stars will burn out. Many astronomers think the answer lies somewhere in between: the Universe will stop expanding, but will not collapse.

▼ *Radio "pictures," like this one, are created by radio telescopes that gather invisible radio rays given off by stars.*

▲ *A small galaxy smashes through the center of a larger one 500 million light-years from Earth. Billions of new stars will be born as a result.*

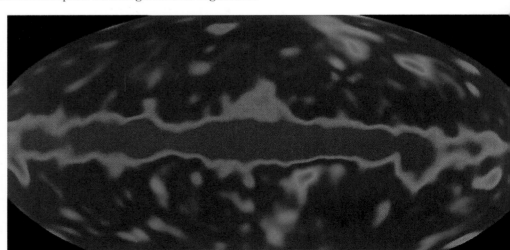

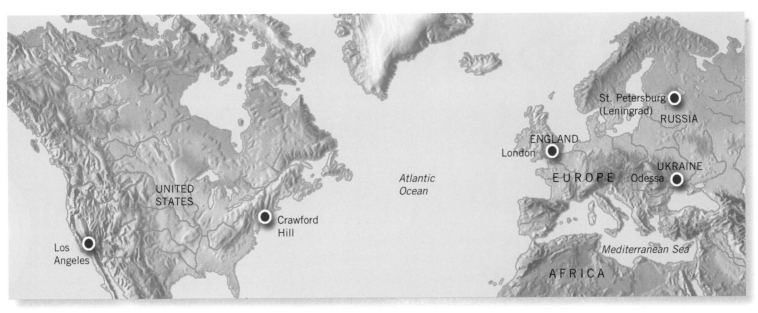

Worldwide Discoveries

Edmund Halley lived in London, while Arno Penzias and Robert Wilson worked for the Bell Laboratories in Crawford Hill, New Jersey. George Gamow was born in Odessa and studied at Leningrad University. Edwin Hubble's telescope was on Mt. Wilson, near Los Angeles.

◀ *In the Big Bang* ❶, *energy and matter were formed* ❷. *This quickly expanded and cooled, forming atoms* ❸. *The atoms came together* ❹ *to form satrs and galaxies* ❺, *which will continue to fly apart for the foreseeable future* ❻.

▲ *This photograph was taken by the crew aboard the space shuttle* Discovery *on April 25, 1990. The Hubble Space Telescope is being deployed after having been prepared in space.*

▶ *The largest possible radio telescopes are used to detect the faintest traces of invisible light at the far edges of the known Universe.*

GLOSSARY

A

Alchemy A medieval philosophical science, the forerunner of chemistry, that attempted to change ordinary metals into gold, to discover a cure for all diseases, and to find a means to prolong life.

Amino acid One of a group of simple biological molecules made of carbon, hydrogen, oxygen, and nitrogen. Amino acids link up to form proteins.

Ammonia A colorless, strong-smelling gas, important in industry. It is used to make fertilizers, explosives, and dyes.

Anatomy The study of the structure of living things. Doctors study the structure of the human body, zoologists and vets study other animals, and botanists study plant anatomy.

Anesthetic A drug that stops nerves from transmitting pain and feeling.

Antibiotic A substance that destroys bacteria in the body. Antibiotics have made it possible to control – and in some cases to virtually wipe out – fatal bacterial diseases, such as typhoid, cholera, and smallpox.

Antiseptic Chemicals that destroy bacteria and other germs, usually on the skin but also in wounds.

Atom The smallest part of an element. Atoms can exist either alone or in combination with other atoms, when they are said to form molecules. Atoms consist of a nucleus made up of protons and neutrons, which is surrounded by orbiting electrons.

B

Bacteria (sing. **bacterium**) Single-celled microorganisms that are either round, spiral, or rod-shaped, and that live in soil, water, organic matter, or the bodies of plants and animals.

Biodegradable When a substance can be broken down into harmless products by microorganisms.

Bond The mutual attraction between two or more atoms when they form molecules.

C

Cathode A negative electrode.

Cell The smallest unit of an organism that can function on its own.

Chain reaction A series of reactions, each of which is started by the previous one. An example is a nuclear reaction, in which a neutron in one atom collides with another atom and causes further neutrons to be produced, which in turn cause other nucleii to split.

Charge The force between particles that either attracts them or repels them. If you brush your hair and it crackles, that is an example of an electric charge.

Chromosome One of the microscopic structures, arranged in pairs in cells, that control genetic information. Chromosomes are made up of genes, which are each responsible for particular characteristics, such as eye color.

Climate The weather conditions in a region over a long period of time – at least 50 years. These conditions include temperature, rainfall, and sunshine.

Combustion A chemical reaction in which a substance combines with oxygen to produce energy in the form of heat.

Compound A substance that contains atoms of two or more elements.

Constant A number or value that does not change. For example, the ratio of the circumference of a circle to its radius is constant.

Continent A large landmass that rises above the ocean floor. The seven continents are North America, South America, Asia, Africa, Europe, Australia, and Antarctica.

Continental shelf The gently sloping part of a continent at its edge, that usually slopes steeply to the ocean floor.

Corrosion The effect of chemicals (in the form of liquids or of gases) gradually reacting with and destroying the surfaces of materials such as metals. For example, oxygen corrodes iron by combining with it to form iron oxide (rust).

Crystal A structure in which atoms are joined in a regular lattice pattern. Salt, sugar, and diamonds are examples of crystals.

D

Diffraction The spreading or bending of waves of any sort – such as light, sound, or water – as they pass through a slit or past the edge of a barrier. A straw in a beaker of water looks bent because of diffraction.

DNA (Deoxyribonucleic acid) The chemical that makes up chromosomes in cells. DNA is able to replicate itself in order to transmit genetic informaton from parent to offspring.

E

Eclipse An eclipse occurs when the Sun or Moon temporarily obscures the other as seen from the Earth. Either the Moon passes between the Sun and Earth, partly or totally blocking the Sun's light (a solar eclipse), or the Earth's shadow falls on the Moon (a lunar eclipse).

Electrode The terminal (metal end point) of a battery, or any piece of metal or carbon that collects or releases a flow of electrons in an electric circuit.

Electromagnetic spectrum The range of radiation made up of electric and magnetic fields, which comprises radio waves, microwaves, infrared radiation, visible light, ultraviolet radiation, X-rays, gamma rays.

Electron A particle with a negative charge that orbits the nucleus of an atom.

Element A substance in which all the atoms are of the same kind and cannot be broken down into more simple substances. There are 92 naturally occurring elements on or in the Earth, each with slightly different atoms. Gold, carbon, mercury, and lead are examples.

Energy The power that enables things to work. It comes from many sources, such as sunlight, food, and fuels like coal and oil. Plants and animals use it to grow, move, and reproduce.

Evolution The gradual process by which animals and plants develop from earlier life-forms. According to Darwin's theory of the "survival of the fittest," in each generation those best adapted to their environment survive.

F

Field The presence of a force around an object, which can act on others. Gravity, electricity, and magnetism all produce fields.

Fossil The remains of bones, shells, footprints, or leaves preserved in rocks. Fossils provide evidence of the existence of animals or plants that lived long ago.

Frequency The rate at which something repeats itself: the frequency of a wave is the number of waves that occur every second.

Friction The force that tends to stop objects sliding past each other. For example, if you try to push a heavy object across the floor, you have to push hard to overcome the friction between the object and the floor.

G

Gene A section of a chromosome that determines an individual characteristic. Genes are composed of DNA.

Geology The study of the Earth and the rocks of which it is made, including how rocks were formed and how they have changed.

H

Hemisphere One half of a globe. The Earth can be divided into the Northern and Southern hemispheres, divided by the equator– the imaginary line that runs around the middle. It can also be divided into the Eastern and Western hemispheres, either side of the Prime Meridian, an imaginary line that runs from the North to the South Pole through Greenwich, in London, England.

Hydrocarbon A chemical compound consisting only of hydrogen and carbon. Petroleum and methane are examples of hydrocarbons.

I

Image orthicon A television camera tube in which electrons scan a scene line by line. Light falling on a screen produces electrons, which hit a second screen, building up an electrical signal from which the picture can be reproduced.

Impurity An impure substance mixed with a pure material. Tiny amounts of impurity are added to a pure semiconductor, crystal, in order to control its electrical conductivity.

Infection An invasion of the body by microorganisms. Infection causes diseases that spread from one body to another by bacteria, fungi, viruses, or by other microorganisms.

L

Latitude The distance north or south of the equator, measured as an angle, of any point on the globe. The angle is measured from the equator to the line of latitude. The equator is $0°$ while the North Pole is $90°$ North and the South Pole is $90°$ South.

Light-year The distance traveled by light in a year. It is equal to 6 trillion miles (9.5 trillion km).

Longitude The distance east or west, measured as an angle, of the Prime Meridian, a line that runs north to south through Greenwich, in London, England. New York, for example, is $74°$ West.

M

Magnetism The name given to the force that attracts some materials to each other and causes other materials to be repelled by each other. Magnetism is also the name for the forces that act between electric currents.

Matter A material substance that has mass, occupies space, and is chiefly made up of atoms. Matter is what makes up the observable Universe.

Meteorite A lump of iron or stone from outer space that is large enough to land on Earth without burning up in the atmosphere. Some meteorites are tiny particles, while others weigh as much as 200 tons.

Middle Ages The time between the fall of the Roman empire at the end of the 5th century A.D. and the flowering of arts and sciences in Italy (known as the Renaissance) in the 15th century.

Molecule The combination of two or more atoms. Molecules form elements or compounds.

N

Neutron A particle with no electrical charge in the nucleus of an atom.

O

Oceanography The study of the oceans and the ocean floor. Oceanography includes study of the oceans in the past and present, as well as shorelines, sediments, rocks, plants, animals, tides, and currents.

Orbit The path taken when one body in space circles another.

Ore A rock that contains minerals from which metals can be extracted. Tin and iron are common ores.

P

Particle A tiny piece of matter that can only be seen through a very powerful microscope.

Patent An official document that gives an inventor the right to charge others to use his or her invention and that prevents others from calling that invention their own.

Photon A single particle of electromagnetic radiation, such as light.

Physics The scientific study of matter and energy and how they interact with each other.

Plate tectonics The theory that the Earth's surface is made of a number of separate, slowly moving plates of rock. The plates float on a layer of molten rock, called the mantle. Mountain chains, earthquakes, and volcanoes are all caused by the moving plates.

Protein A large molecule that makes up a large part of the solid material in animals, such as muscles. All organisms need proteins in order to grow and to repair themselves. Proteins are found in foods such as meat, fish, eggs, cheese, and beans.

Proton A positively charged particle in the nucleus of an atom.

Q

Quantum The smallest "bundle" of energy that can exist by itself. It applies to the energy given off by subatomic particles.

R

Radiation A form of energy, such as light or heat, or particles (such as electrons) coming from – radiated by – an object.

RNA (ribonucleic acid) Chemical present in the nucleus of all cells which, with DA, helps control heredity and growth. One type of RNA controls the manufacture of essential proteins in the body.

S

Substance An amount of any particular material.

Supersonic Faster than the speed of sound – 1,086 feet (331 meters) per second, or 740 miles (1,192 kilometers) per hour. The first supersonic flight was made by Captain Charles Yeager in a Bell XS-1 rocket-powered aircraft in 1947.

U

Universe All of space and everything in it. Astronomers believe that it was formed after the Big Bang, which probably took place 15,000 million years ago. The Universe has been expanding ever since.

V

Vacuum A space in which there is no air or any other kind of gas. Foods, such as coffee, which become stale when exposed to air, are "vacuum packed" in a packet from which the air has been removed.

Virus A tiny organism that invades cells and changes the genetic material inside so that the cell itself begins making more viruses. Most viruses cause disease in animals and plants.

W

Wavelength The distance between two waves of any kind, such as light or sound, from the crest of one to the crest of the next. Light and sound waves of a high frequency have short wavelengths.

Index

A

Africa 6-7, 34
air 28-29
aircraft 17, 52-53
alchemy 9, 92
Alcock, John 52
Aldrin, Edwin 87
Alhazen 22, 23
alphabet 42
aluminum 17
el-Amarna 19
amino acids 92
ammonia 92
anatomy 68, 92
anesthetics 80, 92
animals, domestication 12
antibiotics 6, 68, 78-79, 92
antibodies 79
antiseptics 80, 92
aqueducts 9
Arabs 43, 45, 46, 58, 85
Aristotle 9, 25
Armstrong, Neil 87, 88
Asia Minor 16
Assyrians 7
astronauts 25, 86-87
astronomy 14, 83-85
Atlantic Ocean 46, 52, 60
atmosphere 28-29
atoms 6, 11, 26-27, 30, 38,
    91, 92
Aurora Borealis 20
Avery, Oswald 77
ax heads 7

B

Babylon 14, 84
Bacon, Francis 34
bacteria 68, 70, 78, 79, 92
Baird, John Logie 60, 61
bar codes 37
Becquerel, Henri 32
Bell, Alexander Graham
    56
Benz, Karl 50
Bessemer, Henry 17
bicycles 6, 54-55
Big Bang 90-91
biodegradable 31, 92
bionic people 31

Blériot, Louis 52
Boardman, Chris 55
body scanners 33
bond 30, 92
books 41, 44, 45
brain 67, 69, 80
Braun, Werner von 86
Britain 23, 25, 26, 27, 29,
    30, 48, 59, 61, 62, 77, 79,
    81, 91
bronze 16
Brown, Arthur 52

C

Cabot, John 47
calendars 14-15
camera obscura 22, 58
cameras 58-59
carbon 27, 30
carbon dioxide 28, 29
cars 50-51, 65
cathode 26, 32, 61, 92
cave paintings 6, 42
cells 67, 68, 70-71, 92
CERN 27
Chadwick, James 26
Chain, Ernst 79
chain reaction 38, 92
charge 27, 92
Chernobyl 39
China 8, 14, 21, 43, 44, 45,
    46, 68, 84, 86
chromosomes 70, 75, 76,
    92
Clarke, Arthur C. 88
climate 92
clocks 14
COBE 90
color 22, 23
Columbus, Christopher 16,
    47
combustion 50-51, 92
comets 24
compact discs 36, 64
compasses 20, 46, 47
compounds 92
computers 41, 62-3, 64-65,
    88
continental drift 34-35
continental shelf 92
continents 34-35, 92
Copernicus, Nicolaus 84
copper 16

corrosion 16, 92
cosmology 83
Crick, Francis 76, 77
crop rotation 13
Cross, Charles 30
crystals 92
cuneiform 42, 43
Curie, Marie 32, 33
Czechoslovakia 85

D

Daguerre, Louis 58, 59
Daimler, Gottlieb 50, 51
Dalton, John 26, 27
Darwin, Charles 72-73
Davy, Sir Humphry 80, 81
de Forest, Lee 60
Democritus 26
Dias, Bartholomew 47
diffraction 92
digital technology 64-65
diode valves 60, 62
disease 67, 69, 78-79
DNA 75, 76-77, 92-93
Drais, Baron Karl de 54
drugs 68, 69
Dunlop, John 54

E

Earth 20, 24, 28-29
Eastman, George 58, 59
eclipse 93
Edison, Thomas 57, 58
Egypt 8, 12, 13, 14, 15, 18,
    19, 42, 43, 44, 46, 68, 80,
    84, 85
Einstein, Albert 36, 37, 39
electricity 11, 20-21, 41,
    60, 62
electrodes 93
electromagnetism 21, 27,
    32, 60, 93
electron microscopes 70
electronics 62-63
electrons 20, 26-27, 32, 62,
    93
elements 11, 26, 33, 93
endoscopes 37, 81
energy 22, 23, 36, 38-39,
    48-49, 93
engines 50-51, 52
Euphrates, River 12, 42
Europe 16, 44, 46
evolution 72-73, 93
explorers 47

F

Faraday, Michael 21
farming 12-13, 14, 88
Fermi, Enrico 38
festivals 15
field 20, 21, 93
films 58-59
fire 6, 11
Fleming, Alexander 68,
    78, 79
Fleming, John A. 60, 61
Flemming, Walther 70
flight 52-53
Florey, Howard 79
food 12
Ford, Henry 51
fossils 93
France 29, 33, 54-55, 59,
    79
frequency 93
friction 93
fruit 12

G

Gagarin, Yuri 86
Galápagos Islands 72, 73
Galen 68, 69
galena 16
Galileo 14, 24, 25, 84, 85
Gama, Vasco da 47
Gamow, George 90, 91
gases 28
Gates, Bill 63
generators 21
genetics 67, 70, 74-77, 93
geology 93
Germany 33, 50, 61, 70, 86
glass 11, 18-19
Goddard, Robert 86
gold 17, 27
gravity 11, 24-25, 27, 84
Greece 8, 14, 20, 25, 42, 43,
    46, 48, 68, 69, 84, 85
Gutenberg, Johannes 44,
    45
gyrocompasses 47

H

Hahn, Otto 38
Halley, Edmund 91
Harvey, William 68
hemisphere 93
hemophilia 75
Henry, Joseph 56
Hero 48
Herschel, William 84

Hertz, Heinrich 60, 61
hieroglyphs 42
Hippocrates 68, 69
Hittites 16
Holland 23, 70
Hooke, Robert 70
Hubble, Edwin 90
Huygens, Christiaan 14,
    22, 23
Hyatt, John 30
hydrocarbons 93
hydrogen 28, 30
hydroponics 13

I

ideas 8, 41
image orthicon 93
impurity 93
India 46, 80, 84
Indus Valley 8, 43
Industrial Revolution 49
infection 78-79, 93
internal-combustion
    engines 50-51
Internet 41, 65
iron 13, 16, 17, 20
irrigation 12
Israel 12
Italy 18, 25, 61, 69, 85

J

Jenner, Edward 78, 79
jet engines 52
Johnson, Amy 52
Jordan, River 12

K

Kepler, Johannes 84, 85

L

lasers 11, 36-37, 64
latitude 93
Lavoisier, Antoine 28, 29
Lebanon 12
Leeuwenhoek, Anton van
    70
Lenoir, Etienne 50
Leonardo da Vinci 68
Levassor, Emile 51
Levene, Phoebus 76
levers 7
Libya 42

light 11, 22-23, 36-37
light year 93
Lindbergh, Charles 52
liners 47
Lippershey, Hans 84
Lister, Joseph 80
lodestone 20
longitude 93
Lumière brothers 58
Lyell, Charles 72

M

McCarty, Maclyn 77
Macleod, Colin 77
Macmillan, Kirkpatrick 54
Magellan, Ferdinand 47
magnetism 6, 20-21, 34, 46, 60, 94
Maimann, Theodore 36
maize 12
Malthus, Thomas 72
Marconi, Guglielmo 60, 61
matter 26, 94
Maxwell, James Clerk 60, 61
Mayan Empire 14-15, 43, 85
Mayback, Wilhelm 51
medicine 37, 67, 68-69, 78-81
Meischer, Friedrich 76
Mendel, Gregor 74
Mercedes-Benz 50, 51
Mesopotamia 8, 12, 14, 18, 42, 43
metals 11, 16-17
meteorites 94
Michaux, Pierre 54
microchips 62-63
microscopes 68, 70
Middle Ages 44, 94
Middle East 12, 16, 42
migrations 7
Milky Way 22
Mohenjo-daro 8
molecules 30, 94
Moon 24, 25, 84, 85, 86-87
Morgan, Jason 34
Morgan, William 74
Morse Code 56, 60
mountains 34

N

navigation 46-7
neutrons 26, 32, 38, 94

New Mexico 39
New York 17
Newcomen, Thomas 48
Newton, Sir Isaac 22, 23, 24, 25, 84
Nightingale, Florence 69
Nile River 12, 44
North Pole 20, 34
nuclear power 11, 38-39

O

oceans 35, 84, 94
oil 30
optical fibers 18
orbit 25, 84, 94
ores 16, 94
Otto, Niklaus 50
oxygen 11, 27, 28-29

P

Pacific Ocean 46
paintings, cave 6, 42
Panhard, René 51
paper 44-45
papyrus 44, 46
Parkesine 30
particles 27, 32, 94
Pasteur, Louis 78, 79
patents 94
pendulum 14
penicillin 78, 79
Penzias, Arno 90, 91
photography 58-59
photons 27, 32, 36, 94
photosynthesis 28, 29
physics 94
pictograms 42, 43
Pilkington 18
planets 14, 24-25, 83, 84-85, 90
plants 12-13, 29
plastics 11, 30-31
plate tectonics 34, 94
plows 12
Poland 33
Polynesians 46
Priestley, Joseph 28, 29
printing 41, 44-45
protons 26-27, 32, 94
Ptolemy 85
pure 94
pyramids 85

Q

quantum 94

R

radiation 23, 32, 36, 91, 94
radio 23, 41, 60-61, 64, 88
radioactivity 11, 32-33, 38
railways 41, 48-49
rockets 86
rocks 34, 35
Roentgen, Wilhelm 32, 33
rollers 7
Romans 8, 9, 18, 19, 42, 43, 46, 48
Rosetta Stone 42
Rutherford, Ernest 26, 27

S

Samarkand 45
satellites 41, 47, 56, 57, 83, 88-89
Savery, Thomas 48
Schleiden, Matthias 70
Schwann, Theodor 70
scribes 8
Sheele, Carl 28
ships 46-47, 49
Silk Route 21
Simpson, James 80, 81
Skylab 89
skyscrapers 17
societies, early 8
solar system 84-85
solenoids 21
South America 34, 73
Soviet Union 86, 87, 88-89, 91
space shuttle 86, 91
space travel 86-87
Sputnik 1 86, 88, 89
Starley, James 54
stars 14, 22, 83, 84, 90
steam power 41, 48-49
steel 17
Stephenson, George 48
stone tools 6
Stonehenge 7
Strassman, Fritz 38
subatomic particles 27, 32
substance 94
Sumerians 8, 12, 42
Sun 22, 242-5, 29, 83, 84, 85, 90
sundials 14
supersonic 53, 94

surgery 36, 37, 68, 80-81
Switzerland 37
Syria 12, 19

T

Talbot, William Fox 58, 59
telegraph 41, 56-57
telephone 41, 56-57, 63, 64, 65, 88
telescopes 83, 84, 90, 91
television 23, 41, 60-61, 64, 88
Thailand 16
Thomson, J.J. 26, 27
tides 25
Tigris, River 12, 42
time 14-15
tires 54
tools, early man 6, 7, 11
Townes, Charles 36, 37
transistors 62-63
transport 41, 50-55
Tsiolkovsky, Konstantin 86
turbines 20

U

Ukraine 39
Universe 83, 84, 90-91, 94
uranium 38
United States 30, 36, 37, 48, 49, 56, 59, 62, 65, 74, 77, 86, 88-89, 91

V

vaccination 78-79
vacuum 94
Venice 18, 19
Vesalius, Andreas 68, 69
Vespucci, Amerigo 47
viruses 67, 78
volcanoes 35

W

water 9, 12, 28-29
water clocks 14
Watson, James 76, 77
Watt, James 48
wavelength 94

Wegener, Alfred 34
Wells, Horace 80
Whittle, Frank 52
Wilson, Robert 90, 91
Wright brothers 52, 53
writing 41, 42-43

X

X-rays 23, 32, 33, 69, 90

Y

Young, Thomas 23

Z

Zworykin, Vladimir 61